MW01520023

Born FOR *This!*

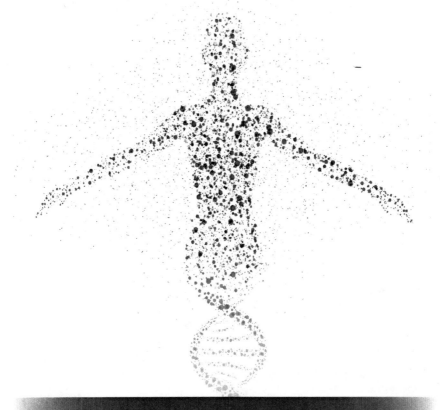

THE JOURNEY TO SUCCESS IN LIFE, LOVE AND BUSINESS

Compiled by

LILLIAN OGBOGOH

Born for This – The Journey to Success in Life, Love and Business

Copyright © 2015, Lillian Ogbogoh

All rights reserved worldwide.

No part of this book may be used or reproduced in any manner without written permission. This publication is protected under the US Copyright Act of 1976 and all other applicable international, federal, state and local laws, and all rights are reserved, including resale rights.

CM Publisher
c/o Marketing for Coach, Ltd
Second Floor
6th London Street
W2 1HR London (UK)

www.cm-publisher.com
info@cm-publisher.com

ISBN: 978-0-9929876-6-4

Published in UK, Europe, US and Canada

Book Cover: Csernik Előd

Inside Layout: Csernik Előd

Table of Contents

Introduction

When I said that I wanted to curate a book bringing together men and women to share their stories of where they had hit a wall, fallen down and the steps that they used to recover, I was met with my own objections. No one wants to admit to failing, let alone talking about it out in public, let alone airing it for the world to see.

I sat back and thought is this really truly? Some of the greatest people who achieved a level of self-mastery failed not once or twice but numerous times on their way to becoming the accomplished heroes we celebrate today. I thought about Edison, Col Sanders and even Mark Victor Hanson and I was spurned to find 26 other people, women and men who were willing to co-create with me a book that shows setbacks are a part of life and the reader is not alone in what they are going through by telling their stories powerfully about their own journey to success.

It was amazing to find people who did not just understand my vision, but who celebrated this aspect of truth telling in our world today. There seems to be a fixation on overnight success, with Facebook and Twitter fueling this idea that everyone has it going on but you. The men and women who have joined me in creating this book span 5 continents of the globe and what ties them together is the veracity to motivate and inspire others to attain their deepest desires by moving through their failures to come out on the other side.

My favorite quote is by Jet Li who said it took him 10 years to be an overnight success. My reason for writing this book is to inspire and motivate you from your space of comfort, apathy, resistance and fear to create a life you love.

Go beyond your fear of failing to see it as a vital lesson on your path of falling forward towards success.

Lillian Ogbogoh

My Deepest Gratitude

This book could not have arrived at this point without some incredible people in my corner, supporting me and this creative process. There are so many people to thank; I can only try to honor you all. Firstly I want to thank my family for their incredible support of my journey and my full becoming. I could not have fully risen to the challenge of creating this incredible project without having Kuumba Nia in my corner, talking me back from the ledge too many times to count. Thank you for being my speed-dial sister and friend.

If this book were a child, Deji Dj Sobanjo would be its godfather! Deji, I cannot begin to thank you for supporting the co-creation of this incredible book and being my go-to person with my random questions and midnight ramblings. Mark Bowness, thank you for seeing my vision, the why behind the book and saying "yes" to making sure it comes to pass. To my incredible partners in the book, thank you for helping me birth this vision into the world!

To my awe-inspiring legendary co-authors, I want to acknowledge each and every one of you for helping me birth this incredible offering into the world and for sharing your powerful stories with such candor and vulnerability. I honor each and every one of you.

And last but not least, I have to thank the incredible team behind the creation of this book, Christine Marmoy! Thank you for being there along the creative journey. From the incredible graphic artists who designed the most exquisite cover for the book to the fantastic editor.

An extra special thank you is given from the bottom of my heart to the fantastic book coordinator and project ninja Celeste Johnson. Thank you for keeping us creative bunch in line and on time.

Co-Author Introductions

KOJO BONTI AMOAKO

I invited Kojo to join the project because this is a man who understands about failing forward on your journey to success – something he discovered on his quest to build a radio station and platform to get others seeing and thinking differently in their day-to-day lives. I could not imagine creating a book that spoke about rising after falling without including Kojo.

JAY BONGO

When I decided to create a book that included men, I wanted to attract men who understood the journey of being a phoenix in their own lives and would be willing to tell it from a place of honesty, passion and true vulnerability. I knew I had to get Jay Julian Bongo as one of my male authors. He is a truly passionate individual who is constantly seeking what makes people great.

KUUMBA NIA

I have the distinctive pleasure of calling her friend and sister. Kuumba is such an incredible woman – a trainer, a healer and a reflective person who sees the greatness in people and reflects it back to then. When I came to her saying that I wanted her in my book anthology she smiled and just said okay.

STEVE G. JONES

I have known of Steve for a while, he is the first person I found that made NLP and its tools easy-to-understand and accessible. He was very pivotal in the changes I made in my life; I became a certified qualified NLP practitioner through his work. I knew that he would be perfect to feature in the book, as he understands intrinsically what it takes to recover after falling down in life.

DJ DEJI SOBANJO

I have known Deji for several years. His vision and insight are just incredible. His passion for helping people was clear in our brief meeting way back then, and we stayed through Facebook. After I explained my vision for this book, his first response was, "What do you need from me to help bring this vision to life?" His passion for the book and the help he has extended to helping the book reach this stage have been absolutely amazing.

AMANDA EPE

I was introduced to Amanda through Deji and I just felt the fire behind this woman, who is a trailblazer with a story to tell and who wanted to share that story with others, to be a compass for others who may be going through the very same things she experienced. She is a woman after my own heart who is passionate about raising the self-esteem of women and young girls, and I knew I had to get her into the book.

JULIE BARNES

I connected with Julie through LinkedIn. The first thing that was apparent from our first Skype chat was her abundant energy and passion. There is an effervescence about her that was just infectious and exhilarating, and I knew that she would be an incredible addition to the book.

MIRIAM HOOLAHAN

I was connected to Miriam through a LinkedIn group, and when I mentioned the project, she volunteered. What I love about Miriam is the meticulous way she approached the project and what she wanted to achieve with her chapter. There was a very deep, honest willingness to tell her story and inspire others to take a bold leap.

TOM EVANS

I have known this incredible man for a few years, and the speed with which he crystallizes thoughts and ideas is just amazing. He is considered to be a modern Alchemist and thought wizard, helping others to unlock their own genius. I knew that having him in the book would be an asset to the readers and myself.

MARK BOWNESS

I was introduced to Mark when I joined his Facebook group. He is a powerhouse of an individual whose major passion and goal in life is helping others meet their ultimate desires. Having spent time speaking with him and understanding his story, his desire and what he lives for, I knew having him in the book had to happen.

HANIFA KAHAR

I met this exotic lovely lady in Mark's group. Her wit and way of seeing the world had me in stitches, and when I heard her personal journey, I knew that she would be perfect for the book as her story is powerful and compelling. I have to say, having gotten to know her, it is an absolute privilege having her as a co-author – plus, I have an exciting visit to Singapore to look forward to!

JASON RUSSELL

I encountered Jason through Mark's group as well. This guy is a bundle of energy. His passion is to have people reach the peak of their physical fitness after learning to overcome challenges with his own health and mentality. He now inspires the greatness out of others using their fitness goals as a springboard. He is on my list of Australians whom I adore.

SARA DONAVAN

I met Sara through Mark's group; she's another awesome Australian, and what struck me was her passion and vibrancy. Being a fellow storyteller, I knew that her words would help transform the lives of others.

SHEILA KADEER

I met Sheila through Facebook as well, then connected with her on Skype. Our first meeting was incredible. There was a woman who had taken the worst experience of her life and made it her mission to prevent other women from experiencing the same things. I was totally blown away by her dedication and forthrightness, so I knew that she would be a perfect fit for the book.

ANNE-MARIE BRUNGARD KNIGHT

After connecting on Facebook, it was so funny to learn that this Connecticut lady used to live down the road from me! Her passion, vibrancy and energy bowled me over, and I knew that she and her story had to be in the book.

SANDRA MARIE HUMBY

This woman and I had been Facebook buddies for a few years when I told her about the project. Initially, she said it was not for her, but later reached out to me saying that she was ready to create a book that touched the lives of whomever read it. I love what she stands for and brings into the world. If you ever get a chance, ask her about healing the mother wound exercise that is so sublimely effective.

AVA BROWN

I was introduced to Ava by Kojo, and what amazed me most was the intensity of her energy and the voracious desire for success despite where she came from. I was in awe of her and was delighted when she asked if she could join in. She embodies the concept of this book down to the last letter.

KEMI OYESOLA

This woman understands the journey of falling down and getting back up with flair and style; having restarted her life at a point at which others would have just given up and gone with the flow, she decided to shape her life, not just for herself but for her future generation. Just ask her about her grandson!

JAY KAMARA FREDERICK

What struck me about Jay is her presence; she fills the room with such energy, which is hard to resist. There is just a matter of fact way about her when she gives insight on a person or situation, and she has a way of seeing people's stories and reimagining them in a more positive, encouraging light.

KONSTANTINOS KAPELAS

I met Konstantinos serendipitously on a train now in London. We discovered that we were both heading to the KPI event in London. We connected after the event and he did the impossible: He went from leaning on the fence to completing his chapter in an afternoon. See what can happen from talking to strangers!

NEIL FELLOWS

Neil has this drive to help people step out into the world in a big way, to help change the course of the world we live in. I love that big mission! After bumping into him at an event and telling him about the book, he stepped up in a big way to share his story. That is how I knew he was a good fit for the book.

DR. VENUS WILLIAMS

After finding out about my project, Venus immediately put her hand up to be part of this journey, which is really amazing as she was on the other side of the world and we have never met.

DARCEY POLLARD

Darcey is another Facebook friend from Australia. The one thing I'm learning about Australians, at least the ones I've encountered, is their willingness to dive in headfirst, taking on challenges before breakfast. That is what Darcey did, and I am so glad to have him onboard as a co-author.

REYNA JOE

Reyna is just an incredible lady who understands the need to help others play their lives out differently. She is a multifaceted woman who is a force to reckon with and a regal energy all of her own.

JESSICA BELLARD

After meeting Jessica, her passions were crystal clear to me: her passion for women to return to wellness and her passion to raise her daughters and have a say in their education. But what impressed me most was the trailblazing and never backing down spirit.

LIANA BAKKER

What struck me about Liana is the title of her website: mountainintomoleshills (and her shocking blue hair). This is a woman who lives her life on her own terms, and ill health was never going to keep her from stepping into the world in a huge way, helping others to find their own true path.

Lillian Ogbogoh

As a Sensuality Discovery Specialist I help pleasure deficient women break the mind-sets and thoughts that keeps them feeling unfulfilled, single and invisible in their own lives. I teach them how to take center stage in their own lives to attract the amazing relationships and life they desire.

My work has led me to speak both internationally as well as locally in the UK. I'm also a bestselling co-author of *Success in High Heels,* a book comprised of 30 leading female authors.

www.lillianogbogoh.com

 twitter.com/LillianOgbogoh

CHAPTER 1

I WAS NOT THE ONE

By Lillian Ogbogoh

Do you remember the first Matrix movie, the scene where the Oracle tells Neo he is not the One? Here is a breakdown of how that scene went:

The Oracle: Well, I better have a look at you. Open your mouth, say Ahhh.

Neo: Ahhh.

The Oracle: Okay. Now I'm supposed to say, `Umm, that's interesting, but...,' then you say...

Neo: But what?

The Oracle: But you already know what I'm going to tell you.

Neo: I'm not The One.

The Oracle: Sorry, kid. You got the gift, but it looks like you're waiting for something.

Neo: What?

The Oracle: Your next life maybe, who knows? That's the way these things go.

That entire scene could have been the story of my life. According to everyone who knew me, I was born successful. Even after the doctors at my birth looked at my parents and said I would not last seven days, as I was only 2lbs and 11oz at birth and 3 months premature.

I got mad at the doctors scaring my mother, so I took a dump in the doctor's pocket and I lost 11oz; so I tell me people I had 11oz of crap in me. Right from the start I was hailed a miracle baby, the achiever and the doer.

Fast forward a few years, I found myself at the lowest point of my life. I had created an events company in partnership with my best friend; we did everything right – working on the business plan, creating events targeting women in business to help them unleash their inner success, bringing in other trainers and coaches to mentor these women.

At the end of these events I had women coming up to me congratulating my business partner and me on the amazing event and heralding us as the next big thing to watch hosting transformational events; yet, I felt very far from this success that everyone believed me to be, but I kept on I was the achiever and doer.

You see, the business was failing and we were running at a loss. I put on a grand brave face and kept on pushing and pushing; even when we had moments of success, deep down I knew that this was not what I wanted to do but I kept lying to myself.

Fast forward a few more years and we were facing the end of our business. I decided to walk away. I became an NLP coach, after qualifying as an NLP practitioner. A few short weeks after qualifying, I was asked by a college if I wanted to teach introductory NLP to their adult students. After saying yes I started getting speaking engagements in far-flung places such as the beautiful Cayman Islands and a little more locally like Dublin.

I was still feeling like Neo, that I was not this amazing coach and trainer that everyone thought. I was holding on to a huge secret. I was doubtful, afraid and scared witless. I didn't believe that I had what it took, that I was enough to make it work.

To be quite honest I felt like a fraud, a liar and a fake, walking around with full-blown imposter syndrome. Unlike Neo, I had no life or death situation to compel me to my greatness, so I hid. There was no leaning in.

In fact, I took myself officially out of the game. I went back to being Mr. Anderson, or, in my case, project management analyst for banks.

Every day I went to work I hated myself a bit more for being there. I found myself dabbling with my coaching from time to time, yet I always found myself running back away from it, getting mad at myself for proclaiming that I was just as good as the other people in my field.

I started to tell a series of lies. Do you recognize any of these? I need to get other qualifications before I can have the success in my field. I have to work years under someone's tutelage before launching out on my own. No one will pay me for what I truly want to do.

Some days, I threw in the race and gender card. I was in full blame mode, which was just a way of hiding the imposter syndrome I was living with. Telling me the vilest things when I was alone, which always started and ended with "you are not enough to do this."

By now you can see a pattern emerging: Once I am told I can't do something, I tend to fight to do it. I went back to coaching but played it safe, still afraid to get hurt. I may not have had the sentinels on my butt or a Miss Smith chasing me down, but I did end up dying. Let's just call it the death of the woman who I thought I was.

I had what I will call a "come to Jesus" moment. I had left my client after a session that had given me some incredible feedback. It reduced me to tears – not the pretty crying of gratitude. Nope! It was full-on sobs and wails.

At that point I was working full-time at a job I hated and dabbling in my coaching. I was broken when I realized the truth of the situation: I was not enough! In that moment something broke in me as I heard *The Matrix* scene playing in my head. The last thing The Oracle says, "Sorry, kid. You got the gift, but it looks like you're waiting for something. Your next life maybe, who knows?"

If I wanted to escape my Ms. Anderson persona, one who was afraid to claim her brilliance while leaping tall building in killer heels, I had to die! So that night I let myself go. And don't think it was without a fight! If you are a superman fan, you will remember that scene where Clark Kent and Superman went toe-to-toe; it was brutal.

I know this is sounding a little brutal and intense, but bear with me here. Firstly, I had to face a few truths about who I was. I realized that dabbling was just that: dabbling. I was not going to get anywhere by being part in and part out. I had to commit to my path, which meant taking daily action in the direction of what I wanted no matter how small.

Also I had to stop wearing someone else's shoes. I had been playing it safe and mild, only showing up as who I thought I should be, not who I wanted to be. I was afraid that if I were my true self there would be an earth-shattering Ka-boom!

But there wasn't. I came out of the closet and told my family that my work is about sensuality and healing and reconnecting the woman with her sensual, audacious and powerful self. And no backlash when I came out to friends and the world. It's made a lot of difference.

Secondly, the whole playing small and imposter syndrome that I was ducking and diving from I had to face square on. Whenever the feelings came up, I always found an ingenious way of distracting myself, be it getting a job, zoning out in front of the TV or just pulling the blanket over my head.

Here's what I did: I stopped talking about myself in the negative and being my own Ms. Smith. I chose to be Morpheus and Trinity all rolled into one. I had to love myself and stop comparing who I am with someone else. I realized that comparison is an act of violence.

I was spurred on by Marianne Williamson's quote, "Our deepest fear is not that we are inadequate. Our deepest fear is that we are powerful beyond measure. It is our light, not our darkness that most frightens us." That one lived on the back of my bedroom doors for a whole year. Whenever I had a moment, I reminded myself of why I could not play small and I could not continue to be that old version of me.

Thirdly I had to realize that "there is no spoon," which means that I was the one creating the drama and trauma. And all the stuff that I was using to self-sabotage was of my own creation. I had to stop acting and reacting.

Please don't think that because I have mastered these three steps that I will never have another moment of hiding and failing. Not so. Even the process of creating this book has led me to kill off other parts of who I thought I was. The one who could not lead a team successfully or actually have people who will be interested in co-creating this incredible book with me, let alone say yes.

And it starts with me whispering to myself, "There is no spoon."

Ava Brown, MBA, BBA, Dip Ed.

Ava is an author, speak, trainer and coach.

She migrated to London in 2002 after a traumatic experience in Jamaica. She has recently published her bio *Bamboo & Fern*.

Ava holds an MBA from the University of Wales. Her interests include lounging with family and friends, cooking, travelling and shopping. She is currently working on the second part of her biography *Indomitable Dream*, which will be out in 2015.

Ava hopes to become an advocate for sexually abused children, as well as to open a safe home in Jamaica for vulnerable children.

www.avabrown.org

 **info@avabrown.org**

CHAPTER 2

BEGINNING OF ENDLESS POSSIBILITIES

By Ava Brown, MBA, BBA, Dip Ed.

Having begun my life in St. Elizabeth, Jamaica, my journey tells the story of how I transcended the humble beginnings of a country girl and emerged a corporate queen.

Being the *only one* that attended university of nine children, I spent a lot of time selling mangoes on the streets of St. Elizabeth, as we were poor and that meant going to school often without lunch and shoes. In spite of this, and the unflattering nickname 'Mango Girl' given to me by others, I knew my only way out of poverty was education.

On the train I was pitied at times; however, I wasn't focusing any of this attitude towards me, as at that age, I was very aware of my status but saw myself "as a horse that was not ashamed to carry its own grass" so selling mangoes was my vehicle to upward social mobility. This attitude saw me through the arduous task of gaining a career as a teacher by age 19. It was my first professional job, and it felt exhilarating to earn my own money. Independence felt good, and I totally basked in it. As I look back, I realize that selling mangoes incubated the skills I have honed to become a successful salesperson.

Even at an early age I had an unquenchable thirst for knowledge. I could recall my teachers telling me never to limit myself, as there is potential in all of us. I nurtured these thoughts, and they are ever fresh in my mind. It was this persuasion to achieve my dreams that empowered me to pursue my ambition. I quickly learned to apply myself, and progressively I chipped away at the stumbling blocks in my path. My belief that struggles are only temporary has allowed me to transform my life, and earned me a successful career in business development, writing, motivational speaking, training, and mentoring.

Growing up there was a lack of role models, especially in terms of academia. Looking around the community there were very few successful people to emulate. Many were tenured in recreational sex, raising babies or going to the farm; however, I was determined to make my life an exemplary one, by not following the path but creating a diversion. I had no concept of how I was going to get there, but I knew I yearned for something different. I was always propelled by my desire to escape the poverty and stagnation of my childhood environment.

I have had what many would term a disastrous life. I have known the dark shadows of incest, carnal and sexual abuse as a teenager. As a young mother in my twenties I have been held at gunpoint and raped. This traumatic experience paralyzed my very being, and I had to flee my country of birth, my home, my all, in order to save my sanity.

Upon arriving in the UK I felt utterly disoriented; it felt as if I had been ejected from the safety of my own DNA, all I had come to know and culture. I came looking for mental sanctuary, but the experiences in the UK were laced with harsh realities and many challenges.

In the UK I was often out of work. I was fired from one of my jobs because I spoke out against injustices to other staff. I was a single parent with a very limited support network. At one stage I almost lost my home, as I couldn't pay the mortgage. I faced racism from neighbors that lead me to sell my first home and start over.

I came to the UK as a qualified teacher, but a few years later I was informed that I could not continue teaching unless I acquired a Qualified Teacher Status (QTS). I found it frustrating, to say the least. I had been good enough to teach for all those years, and then suddenly I was not good enough anymore. This was ever so confusing and hard to ingest as I felt the QTS did not determine the quality of my teaching delivery then or previously. The vicissitude of life in the UK cultivated feelings of anxiety, frustration and doubt of a frightening magnitude. I was now once again thrown out of sync and left to find something else to do.

I felt then that I could resort to my US-based business degree, but I became cognizant of the fact that after investing thousands of dollars doing this degree before moving to the UK in 2002, it wasn't accredited and, in essence, I had wasted money I didn't have. I had lost time, which I could never regain. My emotions were all over the place. Here I was unable to teach and unable to get a decent job in the business sector. My initial dream of becoming a barrister flooded my mind, and I was enraged with regret.

It was at this crucial point that I decided to embark on an MBA in the UK. In order to survive, I had done a number of odd jobs, but obviously I wanted more for myself, so I sacrificed and started the MBA. It was definitely one of the hardest things I've ever done; a working mother, juggling studies with paying the bills to keep a roof over our heads and food on the table – it was hard-core. Yet, I developed tenacity, perseverance and courage. I wanted to try and set an example for my daughter and leave a legacy for my children. I did not want them to struggle the way I did. It was a very hard graft, but what choice did I have? I had two pools of thought here, *sink or swim*. Sinking wasn't an option, so I had better swim, and that is exactly what I did. The MBA started opening doors for me, and I was able to land a decent job, though not without its challenges. I was constantly overlooked for promotion and career mobility.

Completing an MBA reflects my can-do attitude, as well as my determination to achieve my goals. Soon after completing my degree, I was featured in a number of newspapers such as *The Financial Times*, *The Guardian*, *The Gleaner* (Jamaican) and *The Voice* with captions such as "From Mangoes to MBA" and "From Country Girl to Corporate Queen." Most recently, I was selected as a finalist in the Fashion Fair Diva Author Woman of Colour 2015 category; this makes me very proud, as I feel a sense of accomplishment especially as my book was published three months prior to that.

When I glance at these headlines, listen to the radio interviews or watch the TV interviews I have done, I am almost transported into another world as there have been times when I have found it hard to reconcile the girl sitting in a meeting with Directors and CEOs to the little girl who walked barefooted to school hungry, and at one stage homeless.

Shortly after this publicity started I went on to publish my book *Bamboo & Fern*, which sums up my life using the metaphor of the bamboo and fern. My childhood experiences gave me strong roots to grow, but made me tough as the bamboo plant, yet like a fern, with a huge capacity for survival. The highlight of my career to-date was when I was invited to be a guest on the prestigious Jamaican talk show, *Profile*. This was a particularly poignant moment for me because I had always aspired to sit in that chair as a young child growing up in Jamaica, but never felt it was possible. Fulfilling this lifelong ambition was a truly special moment for me – a moment I believe would be a heritage for my children.

I am one of life's go-getters. I am ambitious, steadfast, and perseverant. I am highly focused and determined to reach my full potential, regardless of the barriers. Being a positive thinker, I believe that with the right attitude, obstacles can be overcome. One thing is for certain, I don't let life's challenges stand in my way and instead, I seek to find the positive in all of life's experiences, drawing upon them to become a stronger person. I have discovered that life will always have challenges, but it's how you choose to handle them that highlight the victor in you. Life's challenges do not have to kill your spirit. I have come to realize that it's in the hard times that you should have upward thoughts, ideas of how to make the situation work for your benefit. It's not always easy to do; it takes a particular mind-set.

The one thing that I hope you will take away from my triumphant story is to never allow your past and socio-economic background to limit your possibilities. Today I speak to motivate. I write and share my journey to inspire, hoping that I will encourage others to have a similar attitude.

Sandy Humby

Sandy is an Energy Alchemist and Designer, the author of *Rose Alchemy: Rose Oracle for the Heart* and creator of Rose Alchemy, a Complete Holistic Rebalancing Programme. She is a thought leader in the field of Vibrational Medicine and Heart Coherence, helping her clients and those who are drawn to her work to heal through revealing the nugget of gold in their personal story. Sandy offers one-to-one consultations with clients around the world, both in person and over Skype, and regularly shares her Rose Alchemy program in the UK, Europe and the USA.

www.RoseAlchemy.com

 sandy@rosealchemy.com

CHAPTER 3

THE JOURNEY OF THE HEART: SURRENDERING AND THE PATH TO FIND INNER GOLD

By Sandy Humby

My life's journey has taken me from being a wife, a mother, a successful business owner with two retail shops, a busy workroom and high visibility into divorce, bankruptcy and an experience of what I now refer to as "my wilderness years" of searching, of trying to make sense of my life and to heal the deep heart pain, loneliness and emptiness inside which I had hidden away since my childhood. I was searching for myself, to be able to authentically be present in my life and to have the courage to fully open my heart to love.

I was born in the 50's; my mother was a housewife who loved fabric and sewing. My father landed a job with Aston Martin north of London, and they had moved away from family in the south of England when I arrived. They were both passionate ballroom dancers; my mother making glamorous copies of dresses from Vogue and my father with matinee idol good looks meant they cut quite a dash on the dance floor.

I learned very early on that life was not safe and that feelings and emotions were not to be trusted. My father was a strict disciplinarian and emotionally unavailable, as many were from a Victorian upbringing and war years. He liked his alcohol and had a temper that could flare from nowhere, and incidents I can recall from my very young years created fear and trauma for me as a sensitive soul. My mother was a very anxious woman who was never in robust health and was very much kept in line by my father. My childhood was not a settled or happy time for my younger sister or myself.

The salvation in my young years was my maternal grandparents who lived in a small cottage in the middle of the New Forest. My grandfather was a professional gardener with a magical garden to play in and my grandmother was my experience of warmth and unconditional love. My happiest and safest times were with them.

As soon as I could, I moved out from home and found myself in London sharing a flat and going to art college following my passion for painting and photography. I am still not quite sure how it happened, but when my mother left my father I felt duty bound to make sure he and my sister were ok; so I left my path and went back home to keep everyone together.

Once there it seems I fell into my mother's footsteps and without any recognizable qualification in needlework, save what I had learned from her and made for myself, I secured a place at fashion college. Marriage followed soon after and the opening of my own shop filled with unique wedding dresses and evening wear made from fine silks and antique textiles came along a few years later, together with two children.

I loved sitting and chatting to the bride, getting to hear her story, how she had met her beloved, and being the interpreter of her dreams for her day. Good years followed, creative designs and clients flowed; we had a reputation for fine work, which meant we were very busy. We then opened a second shop in a nearby city, and from that one decision the path of my life was to change.

I still remember vividly: I had just left the solicitor's office after signing the new lease and something stopped me dead in my tracks. As I walked along the busy main street heading back to my shop, I felt sick, faint and shivery. I knew deep inside that I needed to go back and tear up the contract documents.

It was 1988 and I chose not to pay attention to the feeling and listen to that wise voice inside. Instead, standing there in the street I had a conversation in my head. I had taken on staff, we had made stock and the advertising was done and we were due to open the new shop in two weeks. I would let people down. I convinced myself that regardless of how nauseous I felt, it was the right decision to keep going with the plans and that I was just nervous because it was a big step and a substantial financial commitment.

In those few minutes I had sealed a pathway that would ultimately lead me to bankruptcy, divorce, splitting the lives of my two children and losing everything for which I had worked so hard to create for 20 years. It actually took another seven years to finally come to that point – seven years of struggling to deal with the result of that one choice.

When the end did come, when I surrendered to that place, when I gathered what remained together, life took me right out of my comfort zone, out of the pattern of a normal family life, out of the familiarity of my little shop with my name over the door to identify myself.

Life took me into those places and relationships where I could explore and find who I really am, to see my strengths, reveal my vulnerabilities and find out how it was my wounded heart and its magnetic calling that had brought to me all of the challenges, opportunities and rich experiences. To heal the aspects of myself that I chosen to work with and master through this lifetime's journey.

What my inner knowing was trying to tell me was be guided from within, trust that gut feeling and listen to the wisdom of your heart. But my heart had been so shut down in my childhood experience, a place where I had not been able to blossom. I finally realized I had become a pleaser in order to stay safe and loved. I did not trust myself or my emotions and this took me into my healing.

I started exploring energy healing and meditation to find answers and comfort. I found it fascinating to explore the world of vibration, color and sound. I trained in Reiki, Pranic Healing, Neuro Linguistic Programming and coaching to add to my toolbox for myself and others. I began to see the patterns emerging that had governed my choices. Patterns of thinking and behavior I had learned from my experience of family in my early years.

I also saw that these patterns are embedded into our homes and can even determine where we choose to live. I often saw that those in therapy taking steps forward and then getting pulled back into the old ways of thinking once they re-embedded into the energy matrix of their home environment. So I extended my knowledge and experience to Dowsing, Feng Shui and House Whispering.

The final piece for me became clear about five years ago when I went to the Alhambra in Granada, Spain, at rose time. I had been drawn to roses for some time and had begun photographing them. I came back from the Alhambra with some wonderful photographs, but had no sense that there was anything particular about that.

A couple of days later there was a small voice in my head, which I listened to. The inner voice said, "We would like you to put 11 of us together and work with us." I had no question, I knew it was the roses for I had already heard them in the Alhambra Gardens whispering "photograph me, no me, and over here me."

So I gathered eleven roses together and one by one they shared with me in meditation how they worked and what specific purpose each one had come for. In the following year I felt a strong pull to go to Rosslyn Chapel in Scotland, and there the next level of the work became clear with three more roses. By this time I had started sharing the developing work and the roses with small groups.

This was followed by three further sets of roses, each group mirroring my personal process of healing, to follow my inner guidance and truth, to allow my heart to blossom and to facilitate that healing for others.

I am now preparing to launch my 45-card Rose Oracle and Book at a major exhibition in London. Interestingly the last time I exhibited in this place was with my wedding dresses; the journey has come full circle.

The rose has woven her message of love right through my life, from my grandmother Rosa Kate, my grandfather's Rose Garden, my sister Rosemary and even the thousands of handmade silk roses we garlanded the wedding dresses with.

The sweet scented rose, she speaks to the heart.

Hanifa Kahar

I am a successful polyglot with nearly 50 years of experience speaking Mandarin, English, Bahasa Indonesia, Malay and the local Hokkien dialect. My pen name is Hanifa K. Cook.

I am well sought after as a Mandarin language for foreign speakers. From school kids as young as 5 years old to working professionals over 50 years old, my language training is transformational and inspirational, as I believe in providing the skills to get the results. My mission is to empower parents in support of health, wealth and education for their kids.

I am also a Director of Avenue-East Pte Ltd., a company which provides digital data solutions, language training and virtual personal assistant services.

www.childhoodspeech.com

 facebook.com/hianniecook

CHAPTER 4

REMEMBERING CHILDHOOD SPEECH CONSTANTLY

By Hanifa Kahar

The year was 1987. If you were with me that night, you would have been awakened by a loud thud from the living room where my father was sleeping. You would have seen my mother, eldest brother and elder sister cradling my father, his head barely holding itself straight on his neck. He looked like he was struggling to keep it up too. He had fallen and landed on the floor after his head hit the handle of our refrigerator door. He was bleeding, the fall had punctured a vein in his neck, and he had suffered a massive heart attack. You would have seen his eyes barely staring right at me as if I was the last person he wanted to say goodbye to. His eyes shut and his head sank. My mum looked at us and with both hands set apart, palms facing up, she announced, "Dia dah meninggal. Dia dah tak ada." Before she announced this, she had whispered in his ears, the Syahadah.

My father gave me an education that he could never afford himself. Being able to speak four languages made me quite unique. I was very good at telling stories and making speeches. I represented my school in inter-school Chinese Oratorical and writing competitions. As a child, I was a television actress in a Chinese education program, and I was interviewed for an article in the Chinese newspaper for being the "Malay student who acts in a Chinese drama." My father was very proud of me. He always displayed our trophies and had framed the newspaper article.

Because I was the only non-native Chinese in my class, I usually found myself being teased for my name and dark skin color. It didn't bother me at all, but I could not understand why it was a big deal for people to keep calling me "black."

But my father's death did affect me. I lost interest in my studies. For many years after his death, I felt empty. Although, I had no problem getting a job because of my skills and ability to speak three languages, I always felt I was missing something. The thought of his eyes staring at me that night kept haunting me. He never framed my exam results, but he framed the Chinese article and my certificate of participation in the Chinese Oratorical Competition. I never understood why he did that.

MY DAUGHTER

I got married in the year 2000 and had my daughter a year later. I decided quite early that she would learn Mandarin and English. However, I was very lost because we were living in Jakarta and it was not the right city to be in to learn Mandarin. Education resources were scarce for this language and the environment was not conducive for learning Mandarin either. Furthermore, I had not read or used Mandarin formally for many years after school. So, in order for me to teach her Mandarin, I had to relearn it and then learn how to teach it.

One day I was reading the Jakarta Post and I saw this ad in the papers: "Teacher wanted, training will be provided." I responded to the advertisement and got an interview. A few days later, the head teacher from the school rang me up. We spoke in Mandarin on the phone. Earlier on, the school director had told her that I was not Chinese. There was a need to hear me speak Mandarin. After 10 minutes of telephone conversation, I was hired. I got a job as Mandarin teacher in the kindergarten school, which was how I got started to teach Mandarin.

The job lasted for about a year. I was told that I was not a good fit for the company, and they had to let me go. I was devastated. Because my daughter was also enrolled in that pre-school, I had to take her out and move her to another school. I found another teaching job nearby so I could be close to her.

WHAT I LEARNED AS A PARENT

When I became a parent, I saw a need to pursue teaching Mandarin as a career option. I also started studying at the Singapore Chinese Chamber Institute of Businesses. I finally earned my certificate in Business Chinese Translation Skills in 2014 and I also started teaching Mandarin privately at primary schools from 2012. My daughter also completed her primary school in 2014.

> There are only two ways a child looks at the world:
> 1. It is right through their parents' eyes
> 2. Right where their own eyes can see
>
> **Hanifa K. Cook**

I wrote that a few months ago. It became clear to me that I had to be a parent in order to understand why my father did what he did. Before becoming a parent, I could only guess from what he had done to my certificates, trophies and newspaper articles – that he was proud of my achievements as a non-native Chinese student. Now I see that he had framed them because it also symbolized his success as a parent. I started learning Mandarin at pre-school, so his plans to give me a good education would have started well before that.

STARTING A BLOG

In 2008, I was invited to a class to learn about blogging. It was to be the start of another phase of my journey as a parent and teacher. I remember searching for a suitable title for the subject I wanted to blog about. The subject was on speech because I knew a lot about speaking four languages. Somehow, my mind kept going back to the certificates and newspaper articles that my father had framed. It was very difficult to decide what name was suitable.

"Start here. One day, this will all be yours." In one of my dreams, someone had told me those words. I started writing. Childhoodspeech, two words made into one, childhood and speech. I searched to see if that domain name was available. It was. I immediately bought it and created the website. And instantly, it became number one on Google and Yahoo, only because no one else had that name.

It was also my daughter who inspired me to start writing on Childhoodspeech and it was also memories of my childhood achievements that gave me confidence to teach my daughter.

REDEFINING SUCCESS

Although the title of my website is "Success With Languages", it is not filled with tools for learning 4 or 10 languages. It is about learning how to succeed as a parent through the eyes of a child. For my father, it was my achievements as a non-native Mandarin student. He did not teach me any Mandarin, but the fact that I did come home with my trophies and certificates was testimony of his parenthood. For me, it was my ability to raise my daughter to speak three languages before she turned 6 and is now a multilingual student. Through Childhood Speech I finally understood who I should be.

REMEMBERING CHILDHOOD SPEECH CONSTANTLY

Who dares to contradict this statement? Everybody has a childhood. You are born to experience childhood first before you become an adult. If you are an adult searching for answers to your problems, you might just find it in the kid inside you. Attend to your inner child, celebrate your achievements and recognize your strengths.

Mark Bowness

At the age of 26 years old Mark Bowness' marriage ended and he tried to take his own life. This moment defined Mark as he grasped the concept that "we live life, once." Only three months later, Mark leased a 200-acre island in Fiji and invited the world to become tribe members. Tribewanted gained worldwide media attention and was featured in 200 media outlets around the globe including *Good Morning America, The Today Show* and *The New York Times*. The concept was filmed for 18 months and became a 5-part primetime BBC show that aired in the UK, America and Australia.

Mark is now a self-confessed life change catalyst who works with a team of 5,500 coaches from around the world to bring life change into every street, city and community.

www.lifechangetherevolution.com

 facebook.com/groups/lifechangetherevolution

 @lifechangehq

CHAPTER 5

FROM SUICIDE TO SUCCESS: HOW TO START YOUR OWN LIFE CHANGING BUSINESS

By Mark Bowness

Imagine waking up in a hospital bed, dazed and confused. As the fog in your mind starts to clear you re-call the events of the night before. There is no easy way to tell you that I tried to end my life. It happened. It is my story. Each one of us hits a low point in our lives. A low point that maybe not as dark as the darkest period in my life, but it's still your toughest moment. Would it surprise you if I told you that trying to wipe my existence off of the face of the planet was the best thing that ever happened to me? Let me tell you why as I reveal to you the three key lessons that my suicide attempt taught me, lessons that resulted in launching my own life changing business, and how you can do the same.

Warning: This content could change your life. I am about to share with you 3 key lessons that set the path to running a global business and, consequently, totally changed my life. If you take action on all that I am about to share with you your finances, relationships and situation will never be the same.

Ready?

KEY #1: LEVERAGE IS THE BIRTH OF ALL CHANGE

At the age of 26 my marriage was over. The moment that my wife walked out of the door was the end of, not only my marriage, but being part of a church leadership team that did not believe that divorce was biblical. I lost my job, my income and my friends. The only option was to move back to the other side of the UK to live with my parents once again. My future looked incredibly bleak and one night I turned to Google and keyed in "quickest and painless way to end my life," and that's what I tried to do.

Waking up in the hospital the next day reflecting on the events of the day before made me realize how I had existed in a "9-to-5 bubble." I recognized that I had lived on this earth for 26 years and yet I had never truly lived. Rings a bell, doesn't it?

In that moment I discovered that life is the most beautiful gift. It's a treasure to play with, to enjoy and to unlock. I realized that whatever happened throughout the rest of my life, I was alive. Nothing that could ever be thrown at me could be worse than not being alive. This fuelled me to not only dream big, but to act big.

Three months later I leased a 200-acre island in Fiji and invited the world to become a tribe member. Online members got to decide how they would develop the eco-island, what accommodation would be built and how we would grow this community. Members then got to escape and visit the island to take part in its growth and development.

My breakdown was the beginning of the revelation of my purpose.

Do you feel like you are struggling?

Are you simply existing to survive?

Do you believe that there is more to life?

Do you hold a secret unfulfilled dream?

Now is the time. I want you to take action.

Action: Locking in the leverage

The life that I was living was one that I didn't deserve to live. I wasn't living life to the fullest. I imagined what my life would look like in 2, 3, 5 years down the track if I continued in that stage of depression – sad, lonely, unhealthy, financially in pain. I pictured how my life could end up, and this image was the visualization that I needed to do whatever it took to change my financial situation.

I want you to grab a piece of paper and write at the top of it "Things I Don't Like About My Life Now" I then want you to write five headings: Family, Relationships, Career, Health, and Money. Under each heading I want you to write a list of words that describe those areas of your life right now, that you don't like right now. After you have written that list imagine how these words that you have used to describe your life would grow and multiply if you don't go ahead and change now.

Now you have the leverage you need to change your situation. Exciting, right? Ready?

KEY #2: CREATING YOUR LIFE CHANGING BUSINESS

What was the main goal of my business in Fiji? To give people the opportunity to get out of the 9-5 and to have a life changing experience. Sound familiar? Of course it does. My business resonated because it was based upon authenticity. I had a profound experience, and if I was struggling with a treadmill way of living then I knew that I wasn't the only one.

Let me share with you something incredibly important: Creating a business that gives you freedom, that brings in finances and that allows you to live the life that you want to live is not as difficult as it seems. All you need to do is be authentic with what you offer.

Right now I am going to show you exactly how you can start your own life changing business. Let's do it.

Action: And your business is...

Your business could be absolutely anything:

- Selling children's clothes online
- Gardening for the elderly
- Creating a new invention
- Becoming a life coach

I want you to seriously understand your heart. Grab a piece of paper, go within and ask yourself these three questions:

a) What is your secret passion, the thing you would really love to do with your life?

It could be travel, it could be spend more time with your family, or it could be to change the world. Whatever it is is totally okay, just write a list and go with it.

b) How could you monetize your passion?

This is the bit where you get creative. What does your passion lend itself too?

Is it a service that you could provide? Gardening, baking, a life coach, for example?

Is it a website that you could create? Selling handmade items, selling paintings or poems for weddings?

Is it something that you could teach others? How to play the guitar, how to sing, how to (insert whatever it is that you do best)

There are many, many ways to make money; all it takes is a bit of creativity.

KEY #3: START AT THE BEGINNING, IT'S AN AMAZING PLACE TO START

You don't need a significant amount of money to invest into launching a business. Want proof? When I launched my business I asked a friend to create the website for free; he happily obliged. I then shared my authentic business vision with the world and the world became captivated.

What's my point? One of the main reasons that we convince ourselves that we should never start a business is because we don't have the funds to invest. That's a lie, we do. I want you, right now, to start building a website for your business. Take massive action now. Don't stop. Get the idea flowing and watch what happens as a result. Here is what we are going to do:

Get a logo: Head to www.fiverr.com and get a logo created for $5.00

E-mail my friend Ian: Ian@ubermagic.co.uk and tell him I sent you. Ian will create you a website for $120

For the grand total of $125.00 your business is up and running.

What next? Post your website on Facebook, ask your friends to share your website link too. Do whatever it takes to get in your first five sales, and when you do, you will realize that everything is absolutely possible.

Have I made it sound incredibly simple?

Yes? Because it is. Way too many people have convinced themselves that they don't have the funds, that it's hard to run a business or that it will never work for them; in doing so, they never realize the full potential of everything that their life was created to be.

Let me be clear here: I am not suggesting that you quit your job. My point is that you start something. When you start to create your own business, energy flows in that direction: you meet new people, doors are opened to opportunities and life and magic happen. It is only once you have taken action and started something that you can then change direction, that you can realize what is and what is not working and you adapt, change and grow. That's the whole point, right?

So, what is the one piece of wisdom I want you to gain from this chapter? Life is amazing. If you are not truly going out there and living it fully, then now is the time to start. Promise me you will?

Darcey Pollard

Darcey Pollard is a success strategist based in Melbourne, Australia, who has helped clients internationally achieve new levels of success in their professional lives. He helps businesses reach their next level by assisting their teams in achieving peak performance through the optimization of individual's mindset and abilities. A person who holds high expectations from both himself and his clients, Darcey is constantly seeking those that are "doing it better" so that he can then learn their principles to success and put these into a system everybody can use.

Darcey can be contacted below:

www.mrdarceycoaching.com

✉ **darcey.pollard@mrdarceycoaching.com**

in **au.linkedin.com/in/darceypollard**

CHAPTER 6

TRUST THE DIVERGING PATH

By Darcey Pollard

You can set goals, dream, speak affirmations and create a compelling vision, but let's be honest, as much as we love to try and control the outcome of the future; there really are no guarantees. There will always be variables that we cannot predict. There is no blueprint that says if you do X you *will get* Y. Decisions that you make in life have inherent risks. Life, for the most part, is like the map in video games – you can see where you've been, what you've uncovered and you can only see a little way ahead, the rest being shrouded in fog.

Because we can't see ahead and we don't know what is coming, we need to trust that we are exactly where we are meant to be in life and that our next move will be the right one, even if it doesn't make sense or we don't have the complete picture.

2005. The year that I graduated from high school. The same year that I realized that I am on now on my own. With the safety and familiarity of the classroom behind me I had to make the daunting decision of what I was going to do with the rest of my life. While most of my friends had ideas of what they wanted to achieve, I had none. I was paralyzed with the possibility of making the wrong choice, so I refused to make any. I went into full-time work and stayed there for many years until the day I discovered, completely by chance, the field into which I felt compelled to enter.

2009. "That looks like something I'd enjoy" I immediately stopped what I was doing and searched the internet to find out how to become what would soon be revealed to me as a life coach. The first link (and the only one I read) was for a coaching school in Melbourne, Australia, and that was it. My new goal was to move 900km south toward Melbourne and to study at this school. How would I do this?

When would I do this? How did I even know if it was for me? What if I hated it? What if I wasn't good at it? I had no idea; I just knew that I had to make it happen.

2010. After a few months of planning, setbacks and failures, I succeeded in moving to Melbourne with no job, one suitcase and into a place with somebody whom I had never met. There was no stability, no sure way of paying bills (just a little savings), only a handful of familiar faces, and I still didn't even know what this life coach thing entailed or if it was right for me. All I had was a gut instinct.

This was the first time I had decided to place my complete trust in the journey, and it was this trust that would support me in many years to come.

A year after my move I had a stable job, a new car, a happy home, an amazing support network of friends, I was enrolled and studying to become a life coach, and for the first time in my life, I figured out that taking chances and just trusting in the process yields amazing results.

2012. I had relocated to take a management position interstate earlier in the same year. Toward the end of 2012 that appointment came to an abrupt and unexpected end. I had to think quickly, refocus my goals and priorities, make extremely precise decisions and take massive action to get myself back on track. I returned to Melbourne 72 hours later with little planning, no job and no money. I had loans, credit card debt and no immediate, permanent place to stay. If I couldn't get a job shortly after my move I'd be in real financial trouble. My first day back in Melbourne was a Sunday, I applied for 14 jobs and the next day only replied to one, I had my heart set on this one job so badly that I refused to schedule interviews with anyone else, I was burning my bridges as I went. Within a week of moving back I had secured a position with a technology giant that paid 50% more than my previous employer, and my training was to begin the following week. Almost like magic, trusting that things would always work out for the better *proved itself once again*.

There are many reasons people stay safe and prefer to settle for mediocrity, perhaps they're scared they'll fail, be criticized or don't believe they're worthy of success. I believe one of the biggest reasons that people do not take risks in their lives is because of the level of uncertainty and the perceived risk that it presents. The majority of these 'risks' are a) fabricated in your mind and b) have such miniscule chance of occurring, that you're probably more likely to be struck by lightning than to have your absolute worst-case scenario come true. The other risks, those real ones – like supporting your family – these are manageable. If you have the passion and the drive to do something, they're all manageable.

Plan as much as you can, understand all of your options, consider your unique situation and take action. There is always a way.

2014. I made a commitment that after years of playing a small game, it is time to step it up and remember that the reason I embarked on this journey was to become a coach. This year made me realize that becoming a general life coach may not be for me, but becoming a coach within the business arena is definitely where I am best suited. Despite beginning this journey with the intention to become one thing, a small tweak in my journey has presented me with an even more fulfilling direction. It is ok to change direction, to fine tune things along the way. Our lives are not fixed. What you do is completely up to you.

I look back over the past years and realize that the risks I encountered were just tests – tests of my mental strength, of how much I really wanted my goals, of who I am, how I handle pressure, make decisions, and how I fair when I leave my comfort zone. Life has this way of only giving you challenges for which you are ready.

My past years have been preparing me for this year, for the biggest risk I am about to take. I didn't see it at the time but I see it now. Using the lessons I have been taught and my belief that I have what it takes (collected from previous experiences), it is almost time to make the biggest leap of faith yet and leave the harbor solo to set sail toward my goals. Leaving the safety of the corporate shore and taking on the open ocean, my business as my vessel. Life is a never-ending journey of risk, and I wouldn't have it any other way.

I am born for my journey, as you are born for yours.

Neil Fellowes

While working in sales, Neil Fellowes was struggling with many things in his personal life including an abusive relationship, debt, obesity and a huge loss of confidence. To correct his life path he immersed himself into personal development and mind, body and spirit teachings. What he didn't know at that time was, not only would he correct his life path, but become a leader in the industry he'd learnt so much from, using his core business skills.

www.7FigureBackOffice.com

facebook.com/7FigBackOffice

uk.linkedin.com/in/neilfellowes

CHAPTER 7

OVERCOMING THE ODDS

By Neil Fellowes

I took two steps inside the room and stopped. Frozen. Shocked. They were oblivious, engrossed in their conversation and had no idea of my presence.

The words shook me. I couldn't believe them. I couldn't believe they were about me. My mouth fell open. My legs buckled. I reached out to the wall for support and doubled over.

There was nothing for me to say. No fight left inside. I backed out of the room as quietly as I entered. Softly, I climbed the stairs. I wanted to disappear, go somewhere I could shut the door and let my emotions flow and still retain my dignity.

Six years earlier, aged 27, I'd returned to college. I just got divorced and sold a business I'd grown five-fold in two and a half years. I had a property I rented out and was 12 stone, athletic and doing okay in life.

The mess my life was in could never have been predicted.

I was brought up in a beautiful house my dad built, in a busy village on the edge of town. My parents were thoughtful, supportive people. At school I never set the world alight with my academic prowess, but on a sports field I could compete with the best. I never sought leadership, but it always sought me. I was a prefect, a games captain, played sports for the county and captained my Sunday football team.

Later at work I went from trainee into sales management in under two years.

But now my life was a mess. I'd lost all the money from the sale of my business, the property I'd once rented was now sold and the profits gone, and I was in debt. I'd gone from athletic to overweight in three years; my knee joints were shot and my back ached almost constantly. Worst of all, the relationship I was in had become abusive, not just verbally, but mentally and physically too.

Back in the bedroom, shut away, my stomach in knots, tears running down my face, I asked myself a stream of questions. How had I let this happen to me? How had my life become so bad? How could my partner speak about me with such venom?

I replayed the words she'd spat out. "He's a fat lazy loser, who has a dream he's never going to fulfill."

That hurt. It hurt. I hurt. I hated my life. I hated the fact her words had some semblance of truth. I hated that I'd allowed myself to sink so low.

I pulled myself together and left the room. I'd only gone a few strides when I overheard my son playing with his toys in the next room. I pushed open the door and ventured inside. There he was bashing his toy tractors together. As I watched him, questions formed in my mind: What does he think of me? Does he think I'm a fat lazy loser? More importantly, what will he think of me in 20 or 30 years?

I didn't like the answers.

I wanted him to look up to me. I wanted to be his hero. I wanted to have achieved something in my life that said, "you can ask me anything because I have my life sorted." But I was far from that.

Something needed to change. I needed to change, and quickly.

Within two weeks I was out of the house. I'd moved back with my parents. At that time I didn't know that I was embarking on a path that would change my life, the life of my kids and many others lives whom I would never meet.

It took almost a decade to change, improve and then transform my life from where it was. I read hundreds of self-help books and I focused on correcting one thing at a time. At first I needed to take care of my health. Without that there would be nothing else. With that on track it took 23 appearances in court over seven years to take care of the welfare of my children before I could happily feel they could thrive.

As I got my children onto a better path, I began a new relationship. With what I'd been through I wasn't really interested in a relationship, but when I met Jo and saw her qualities, I knew I'd be a fool to resist her. That hunch proved right. She's an amazing person who saw the good in me and brings out my best.

About the time I met Jo I began visualizing. I saw myself kneeling on a beach at Christchurch, overlooking the Isle of Wight, having signed for my dream house the day before. I saw the house as a place a few miles from the beach, but in rolling countryside. I visualized farmland, but the animals were not mine. I also visualized that the authors of the books I was reading would become my friends and associates.

A friend invited us to his home in Bournemouth for a weekend. He invited us to go for a walk that took us to the beach at Christchurch. I was kneeling in the sand when I realized I'd been visualizing the moment. As it happened we had travelled to Somerset the day before and signed for a house where we could just see the coast. We have hills all around us, and we live in a house built on old farmland, with animals in the fields behind us.

Dreams do come true, despite what others may tell us!

With my health in good condition and my family life on track, I was finally able to turn my focus to my career. After what I'd been through I wanted to do something that had meaning. I'd struggled for many years and through what I'd learned, I came to realize there was no need for me to ever have struggled in the way I had – and probably no need for anyone else to ever struggle either.

It became my purpose to help other people improve their experience of their everyday lives. Jo was already coaching people and we worked together, setting up our first business together. We enjoyed most of what we did, but knew from early on there was something not quite right with that we were doing.

After some tweaks and changes we eventually stumbled on something that felt right and took off. I'd love to say we planned it, but if I'm honest it morphed into 7figurebackofice.com because I stopped trying to make it be what I thought it should be and started to listen to what the business wanted to do.

As it turned out, it wanted me to pay forward what I had learned about life through reading so many self-help books and the authors, speakers and coaches in that niche reach more people. As in my visualization, many of these people are now my friends, associates and clients.

When you work together and live together you have to work as hard at your relationship as you do your business. Weekends away, dinner together and a date make all the difference. We've also thrown ourselves into Ballroom and Latin dancing. It's enhanced the connection between us and taught us a lot about how masculine and feminine energy can flow powerfully if you feel for each other.

Jo continues to bring out the best in me, and I only ever want to do the same for her.

My top 3 tips:

1. Know what you want. Visualize it and focus on making it happen. I've always found it's better to work on one thing at a time, that way you can give it more attention so when opportunities show up that help you, you can spot them and enjoy them

2. Create a rhythm. When you know what you want, put a daily habit in place that supports it. This puts goal achievement on steroids.

3. Aim to bring out the best in the person you choose to spend your life with and allow them to do that for you.

Dr. Steve G. Jones. Ed. D.

Dr. Steve G. Jones, Ed.D. is a board certified Clinical Hypnotherapist who has been practicing hypnotherapy since the 1980s. He is the author of 25 books on such topics as hypnosis, the law of attraction and weight loss. Steve has also created over 9,000 hypnosis audio recordings and 22 different online certification programs, which are sold in over 140 countries.

Dr. Steve has been featured on Bravo's Millionaire Matchmaker as both a hypnotherapist and a millionaire. Additionally, Dr. Steve has been interviewed on CNN, ABC, NBC and CBS.

Dr. Steve has a bachelor's degree in psychology from the University of Florida (1994), a master's degree in education (M.Ed.) from Armstrong Atlantic State University (2007), a specialist degree (Ed.S) in education (2009), a doctorate in education (Ed.D.) at Georgia Southern University (2013) and has studied psychology at Harvard University.

CHAPTER 8

MY WINDING PATH TOWARD SUCCESS

By Dr. Steve G. Jones, Ed.D.

I have had a few setbacks in my life. I am 46 years old, and I can honestly say I have experienced the ups and downs of life. I fully believe that people can learn from other people's mistakes and failures. I also think it's important for people to share their life experiences with others because when people experience failures, they often feel as though they are all alone. But this is far from the truth. Everyone has experienced at least one failure in their life; the challenge is that few people share their failures with others because of shame, guilt and all the emotions that go along with a failure. I want to share my story with you because I hope it will give you hope and inspire you to move forward with your goals and dreams.

As with all failures, it didn't start out in a negative light. In 1988 I got married to a woman I was very much in love with and had bright dreams for our future. I pictured us experiencing life and its adventures together for a long, long time. I could imagine us being old together. I knew marriage wasn't going to be easy, but I was in it for the long haul. My marriage came to an end in 1996, after 8 years. We filed for divorce and I was devastated.

The next few years after my divorce are sort of a blur. I was depressed for a while, and I had to allow time for myself to grieve and heal. It was hard telling friends and family that we were getting a divorce. I felt like a failure. I had to come to terms with the fact that my marriage failed. And although my marriage failed, that did not mean I was a failure. It took me some time to wrap my mind around this thought, that I was not a failure. I had to tell myself that I would recover and that perhaps like could be better than I had pictured.

Since I got married at a young age, I do not think I had a sense of who I was. Your 20s are a time when you are growing and changing, getting an education, starting a career and really learning who you are. After my divorce, I really questioned what I wanted and began focusing on myself and what I wanted. Everything was new to me. I had to develop a new routine.

During my recovery, I used self-hypnosis and affirmations to make myself feel better. I used them to help build my confidence, to improve my sleep, to distract myself from negative thoughts and to become more motivated to move forward with my life. I first practiced hypnosis when I was in military school when I was 15, but after my divorce was the first time in my life when I started using hypnosis and affirmations to help myself personally. I would record hypnosis sessions and affirmations for myself and listen to them whenever I needed. This was very therapeutic for me. The affirmations helped me consciously think in a more positive way. The hypnosis worked by re-programming my subconscious mind. They helped me feel more confident and positive.

I am sure many of you can relate to divorce. You have likely heard the statistic that 50% of marriages end in divorce. Knowing that other people have been through it does not make it any easier, but it does mean that there are people in your life that you can confide in and they will understand what you are going through. Divorce is so upsetting because it represents the loss of the relationship, commitments made in the past and the future you had envisioned. The important thing to remember during a divorce or after any failure is that you will move on. You will not know when you will move on or how you will move on, but you will move forward with your life.

By 2000, I felt like I was back on my feet. It was at this time in my life that I decided to move from Florida to California. Florida is where I grew up, attended college and where I lived during my marriage. I wanted a big change in my life. I wanted to explore hypnosis, NLP and coaching, and I felt that California was where I could take my knowledge to the next level. I quickly got settled and opened up my hypnotherapy practice in the Roxbury Medical Building in Beverly Hills. I wanted to be in the 90210 zip code and I made it happen.

Hypnosis was much more widely accepted in California, compared to the East Coast. I was constantly going to networking events and made a lot of contacts – people who would refer clients to me – and I also made great friends. I started seeing celebrity clients, actors, actresses, and athletes and was booked solid every day. It was very fulfilling to me, knowing that I had changed my life, focused on something I was passionate about and was helping people change their lives around as well.

It was also at this time when the Internet was becoming an essential part of our daily lives. I started recording hypnosis sessions on CDs and sold them on eBay. I was impressed that I could sell a recording even while I was asleep. People were starting to use mp3s instead of CDs, so I started creating those. Since then I have created over 9,000 self-improvement programs, and in 2013 I received my doctorate degree in education.

Since my divorce, I have had some setbacks in life, love and business, but I learned the most from my divorce. It encouraged me to pursue self-improvement. Because hypnosis and affirmations helped me so much, I thought hypnosis and affirmations could help others. I no longer see my divorce as a failure. I see it as a learning experience for which I am eternally grateful because it brought me to where I am today. It has allowed me to help thousands of other people. I used to only see clients in-person, but now my focus is on recording programs that people can download from anywhere in the world and use within seconds of purchase. It has opened the doors for so many more people to improve their lives.

No matter what failure you have experienced in your life, it is so important to pick yourself back up and keep moving forward. I know it seems impossible, but I am here to tell you that you can do it and life will be better. If someone had told me back in 1996 that this is where my life would end up, first, I might not have believed them, but it would have given me so much motivation and optimism in my life. This is exactly what hypnosis does. It reprograms your subconscious mind and helps you to visualize what your ideal life would look like. Simply by visualizing, you are on your way to realizing your ideal life. I did not know that I would become a world-renowned hypnotherapist. I did not know I would end up helping thousands of people all around the world. However, I believed in myself and I feel that was all that mattered.

Since my divorce, I have not remarried, but I have had some very meaningful and loving relationships. I turned my focus toward my career and toward my passion, which is helping people. My work has grown immensely over the years. I have found solid business partners and great employees, and I continue to educate myself on new topics the latest technology.

I never got to a point where I just stopped and said, "I am content with where I am; there is no need to do any more." I am not satisfied by this kind of outlook. I want to constantly grow, take action and improve my life and the lives of others. This is the main principle I learned following my divorce. It did not make any sense to simply be okay with where my life was at that point. I have taken this outlook and applied it to many other setbacks I have experienced. A setback is simply a learning experience. I like to look at it as the universe telling me that I need to go in another direction.

Amanda Epe

Author of the book *A Fly Girl*, an inspirational and international travel memoir, Amanda's mission is to write, educate and encourage. Since 2000 her calling has been in community education and development and her purpose is to empower girls and women. She is a member of the UN Women National Committee U.K. She leads *Ms Rose Blossom*, a project with services of coaching and educating girls and women in one-to-one sessions and group workshops. Her clients and participants work on self-esteem and sexual health awareness and use writing as art and therapy.

www.amandaepe.com

www.msroseblossom.org

✉ mail@msroseblossom.org

f Facebook.com/amandaepe

f Facebook.com/msroseblossom

🐦 @msroseblossom

in Amanda Epe

CHAPTER 9

THE DREAM CATCHER

By Amanda Epe

I was a happy go lucky Londoner born and raised with all smiles. Young, buoyant and creative until my life took a melodramatic downward spiral. When my peers had successfully completed their undergraduate programs, I had given up. At twenty-one when friends where completing undergraduate courses, there I was a disorientated dropout, divorced from the institution and depressed.

The word "career" was an unnecessary pressure to an experimental creative who was not ready to engage in the academic pathway. There were roads that I wanted to venture and they were unconventional routes – for the dreamers. To write and create educational projects topped with some sporadic travel would be the dream fulfilled.

"Amanda lives in fairyland, why doesn't she realize that lifestyle is out of bounds?"

I had become a laughing stock, and the rumors got back to me, but I still believed in my dreams. In my early and mid-twenties I was gazing around, at times unemployed yet having some hope to engage in exciting media, whilst a college friend already had achieved this role and was employed by the BBC; other peers had become qualified teachers. I procrastinated and only dreamt of writing without putting pen to paper; writing was all done in my head.

Having completed a Higher Diploma in Journalism, the course enabled me to start the writing process and finally have my creative feature published. Still I didn't feel adequate; I was a think tank, full of creativity with no action and I felt like a failure. There were young graduates sprouting out every so often known for writing books, anchoring programs or assistant producing for television, and I was just a dreamer. I couldn't catch my dream as a writer and it was time to explore my other dreams.

It is every girl's dream to travel the globe and capture new horizons. I began to dream new dreams of carefree travel and adventure. One of the best ways I imagined doing this was being employed by an airline. I envisioned being employed by the best to gain the opportunity to visit distant nations and regions of the world, so I set my mind to it.

My first application was to British Airways. Being a perfectionist in completing application forms, I was shortlisted from the thousands of applicants for an initial introduction and preliminary interview day. The vision of travels had come closer; I was floating over the moon. But half way through the day I was sent home, there was no new moon for me. I had failed to get through the activities and I was furious. It took me a vast amount of time to regain my composure, and get over the rejection. But I was adamant I was to fly.

I repeated this process with numerous airlines, was successfully shortlisted but always sent home at half day. Eventually I had an interview day with another top airline and managed to get past the half-day mark. However, in the afternoon I was shown the door. At least if I was a runner up I would receive a medal, but I had come so close and nothing gained. I went home curled up in my bed and soiled my pillow with a pool of salt water, unstoppable tears. I realized how desperately I wanted this as the failure left me deeply hurt from the experience. There was not a chance I could go through that again!

Then I was persuaded by a beloved to respond to an advert calling for Cabin Crew for British Airways. "Not again!" I exclaimed. Having been through their interview day on my first attempt and after my last interview experience, I could not put myself through recruitment procedures for the fear of failure. But I did, and this time I was successful. I travelled the world on long haul routes, resided in luxury, but being unfocused, I failed to catch my highest dream, after all my globetrotting I was not the travel writer I set out to be. Fast forward to 2014.

Leaving the airline and the world of travel, unable to achieve the writing dream it was high time to follow my calling in education work. My first role in the education sector was a Learning Support Assistant. It was rewarding to help young people, yet a fleeting feeling of failure clouded me when I was in the school library. Surrounded by books I knew I also could be writing stories and creating programs for learning. Step by step I took on new roles in education from Learning Mentor, Special Needs Assistant and Literacy Teacher.

I had climbed to the top of the stairs and met success in an opportunity to work in education and international development. I had been selected to work under the auspices of the Nigerian President Goodluck Jonathan in researching and writing education and health programs for the development of women in the state in which Mr. President was the former governor. The benefit of that work was invaluable for me and the community at large. I was able to combine being a writer, an educator and traveler all in one, as well as contributing to change for individuals and having a positive impact on large community groups.

Life in education was transformational. I recommenced my creative writing journey, contributed to anthologies and wrote journalist reports. I also completed an undergraduate degree in education and then followed up with a Master's degree. Building upon previous success by contributing my writing to collaborative works, I was confident in completing my own book, and recently finalized my debut travel memoir, *A Fly Girl*. In addition to authorship, I also achieved another objective of education work; I am delighted to run my own project for empowering girls and women.

In the spheres of writing, education and travel I have caught my dreams and accomplished my unsinkable desires. Enjoying these moments I know I was born for this writing life and I continue to dream of new plots and ending. Regardless of age catching new dreams are not over! I encourage you to adopt my strategies. Below are three of my mandatory actions for building success and the summaries from lessons I have learned.

1. APPRECIATE SELF

In hindsight I realize I have a unique pathway. I was caught up in the notion of age and academic comparison in my twenties. When society determines what individuals should be doing at each age of life, one can feel like they have failed. However I draw from example from my favorite writer Paulo Coelho who started his writing career at forty years and the inspirational author Maya Angelou, pregnant as a teenager, who searched far and wide for her passions in life and experienced many occupations before becoming a bestselling writer. These examples are evidence that we are unique and our dreams manifest at the destined age and stage.

2. DEVELOP SUCCESS FROM SMALL STEPS

Following on from the above, self love and appreciation as the only way forward, I then reflect on my writing path to recognize the small steps. I acknowledge my achievement from my Diploma course and my first published writing, having my works selected for anthologies with acclaimed and award winning writers, to positive reviews from literary journals. This method enabled me to keep on moving, and to set goals to meet success of becoming an author.

3. PERSIST EVERYDAY FOR NEW OUTCOMES

A tenacious Taurus, I may fail, become an angry bull but having my mind set on blissful dreams, I consciously make the choice to see them through. Once the creative visualization is planted I fertilize it and wait for its season to grow.

Dr. B. Venus Williams, PhD

After receiving two Ph.D. degrees which uniquely integrate the fields of physiology and biology with pure and applied mathematics for a deep look into the intricate and dynamic dance of the heart, Dr. B. Venus Williams, Ph.D., fully embraced the fact that everything is energy and chose the quantum path to organic holistic healing and complete permanent health in all aspects of the being and all areas of their life. She inspires and enlightens in harmony with the Universal Laws of Nature. Her advanced energy healing abilities paired with her potent claircognizant skills are gifts to all.

www.VenusRecommends.com

www.YouAreTrulyDivine.com

CHAPTER 10

YOU ARE TRULY DIVINE

By Dr. B. Venus Williams, Ph.D.

My life is a sequence of beautiful manifestations that have the ability to inspire, heal and enlighten. It took me a while to realize this truth. I perceived myself as a victim of a difficult life. The hardest situations turned out to be the biggest blessings for me. I realized that every vulnerability came paired up with an opportunity for manifesting desired results. When I felt most vulnerable, I was given an opportunity to experience my true divinity.

The purpose of my visit with you is to let my life story remind you that you are truly divine and to inspire you to manifest your desires.

I always desired to know everything. I started at a very young age and mastered all knowledge that was available to me. My teachers chose "brilliant" to describe me. I earned many advanced and unique degrees, including PhDs. Up to the moment Angel showed up in my life in the body of a playful puppy.

I was very logical. Every solution came from my left brain. Although, I was shutting off my creative self. I suppressed the connection with my Creator, The Divine, and was brainwashed that creation happens through hard work and learning from outside sources. I was ignorant of the existence and power of my subconscious mind.

My life's journey showed me that all creation starts within me and I am in control of what I create. I realized that the universal power that I call The Divine is within every one of us. It is always available to me at my command if only I know how to connect and communicate with it. Being divine is our true essence.

I used to constantly forget about my divine inner power to manifest my desires. This forgetfulness caused me to feel like a victim, and my body experienced constant tiredness and lack of energy from carrying around all the weight of the heavy black chains of victimhood. The irony was that I allowed myself to be in that position by forgetting who I truly was.

Let me introduce you to Angel: He has been my companion forever. He shapeshifts and chooses different appearances according to what fits the situation best. Right now Angel has chosen to look like a playful puppy.

The angels are free, happy and playful, with a healthy sense of humor. They love to enlighten. They are available to all of us constantly and instantly. They are ready and able to help us remember who we truly are and live happily ever after with this wisdom. We have to ask them for support. Remember that each of us has a free will of choice, and by asking them to guide us, we allow them to help us. We can allow life to be easy and pleasant by asking for their help and gratefully accepting it.

When I met Angel again for the 'first' time in his appearance as a playful puppy, I loved him at once. He came to live with us. I noticed he scratched himself often. We went to the vet who told me that Angel had to be put down. He said that his immune system was genetically and permanently defective. Angel was three months young.

I felt overwhelming panic, tears rolled down my face. My heart was bitterly crying and pounding in my chest like a hammer, but I didn't accept the vet's opinion. I had no idea what to do. If only I could perceive the gift in this situation then.

I was very attracted to the concept of living a happy, healthy, abundant life. I innately knew it was possible. Although I felt powerless at that moment, I was determined to manifest the beautiful life I imagined. I truly desired to live a fairytale. Angel was with me, helping me manifest my fairytale and enjoy living it.

I said "no" to the vet, although I had no solution in mind and no plan of action as to how to heal Angel's body.

What kept me going was my LOVE. I love Angel. And the power of love allowed me to open my mind and heart to believe that everything truly was possible. All second opinions were like the first one, unacceptable to me.

The problem with Angel's body with no outside solution was a great opportunity for me to open up the door to the treasure house of infinite creativity within me and manifest health for him. I clearly see now how every cloud has a silver lining and the cloud shows up for a reason to guide us to our true selves.

The infinite power of true love in my heart let me listen to my inner knowing and ask for guidance. I allowed the door of infinite possibilities from within me to open. I let the Divine be expressed within me, through me and for us. I healed Angel's body quickly and easily when I opened up my heart and mind to my spiritual gifts and inner knowing. This experience activated my infinite inner power for manifesting desired results and completely changed my life.

This happened ten years ago, if we choose to measure time in earth years. Ever since I have been helping others heal through my inner knowing, talents and abilities.

The gift of this experience was that I became aware that I was in control of my manifestations and the same universal quantum laws apply to manifesting anything I truly desire.

It became clear to me that my life was difficult because I wasn't consciously aware of the existence and power of my subconscious mind. I discovered my subconscious mind and its power to easily create what is in alignment with its programs. I became aware that the easy manifestation happens when the subconscious and conscious minds are aligned, and the harmony between them is essential to a flow of easy manifestations. I discovered that my subconscious mind actively participates in the process of creation, and it is essential to release limiting beliefs and faulty programs from it because they interfere with what I consciously choose to manifest and make life difficult.

Here's another example. It was Tuesday, March 18. The morning was beautiful. The fresh air was pleasantly cold. The ground was covered with a foot of virgin snow. The tall trees serenely moved their tops in a beautiful dance orchestrated by the song of the birds who truly enjoyed the sunshine. The sun kissed the surface of the snow with diamond sparkles. Abundance was the best way to describe the power of nature that Angel and I were witnessing. The warm embrace of the sunshine was hugging my body and I felt relaxed and supported. The power of nature opened my heart and allowed the true inner peace from within me to come out and play.

We lived on the top of the hill in a big colonial house cuddled up between the trees. This was during the time when the economy and the real estate market were down. Properties were sitting with "For sale" signs for years, and fear had all at a hold.

On that Tuesday morning, I asked for a clear sign if it is best for us to sell the property and move. I asked, detached from the outcome and let go in complete faith. Then we went inside and sat by the fire.

On Friday of the same week, there was a letter in the mail that attracted my attention at once. I opened it as I walked up the steep driveway. The date on the letter was March 18, the same day I asked for a clear sign and guidance. The letter read, "If you ever decide to sell your property, we would like to buy it." This was very clearly lighting the next step of the way for me. Clear guidance has beauty and power in it.

The people who wrote the letter bought the property. This is how easily and instantly a three quarter of a million property was sold in a market that was frozen, in an economy that was down, with no advertising at all, with no real estate agents, with no traffic of visitors to look through the house and property, with no "For Sale" signs.

I desire that this short visit with you now inspires you to believe in your true self. Have faith in your divinity and its infinite power to create your desires. Trust your journey. I shared with you a few universal truths. I am happy to tell you more. You can find me at YouAreTrulyDivine.com for more inspiration, empowerme

Konstantinos Kapelas

Konstantinos Kapelas a qualified practitioner in several leading health skills (over twelve). He helps others to achieve the same gains he has. This success was the foundation for the Kapelas Health & Vitality System™. He speaks domestically and internationally at events like Mind Body Soul, Festival of Life, VegFest, 4 Networking, as well as giving educational talks for companies. His articles have been featured in magazines such as *Time & Leisure, Families, The Fresh Network, The Green Parent,* and he has co-authored a book called *Successful Living & Successful Marriage,* which it is forwarded by Jack Canfield, a *New York Times* bestselling author.

Specialist in Rebuilding Health & Recharging Energy

www.totalhealthnow.co.uk

CHAPTER 11

PERSEVERING IN LIFE WHEN HOPE IS THE ONLY THING LEFT IN YOU

By Konstantinos Kapelas

It was September 1997 and I had just received a Bachelor's in Tourism management and distinction on my thesis. Although, I was the first one from my extended family ever to graduate from a university, something inside was telling me to go abroad just for the experience.

I arrived in London in November 1997 – my first time in another country – and I knew no one, apart my English girlfriend whom I had met in Greece. Although I was a leader with a strong personality,, it was tough to find myself in the center of London working in a kebab house instead of a good restaurant, which I was promised through my communications prior to my arrival in the UK.

It was very depressing as the staff changed regularly and no one cared for the customers. In addition, my English girlfriend wanted me to move in with her, which meant that I needed to spend all my savings for a deposit and I would not even have money for my flight back. The situation was very difficult as she was new in London as well. We ended up splitting up, which left me completely alone and really hurting inside.

At the kebab house there was another Greek guy who I told that I would leave the country and his reply was, "if you leave you would be a coward." That statement really motivated me to stay, as I was too proud to return back in Greece as a failure.

One day he took me to a park where we played football against people from other nationalities. I scored lots of goals, which caught the attention of a Greek guy who had connections to the London

Cypriot community and their football leagues. I was taken on trial to a Cypriot football team. They were very impressed, wanted me to sign up and help me find a proper job and in return play football for them. I wanted to sign up right away, but the person who introduced me to them had a personal plan B looking to negotiate his interests rather then mine. Eventually, I had to make the arrangements with the football team myself.

They quickly got me a job interview, which went well, and I accepted it without a second thought. However, it was very difficult finding a place to live. For five days I lived in a house under refurbishment with no heating or water in the middle of winter, just my sleeping bag. Then I moved into a room sharing the same bed with another guy for over a month until I found a room to rent in a family home.

I finally had a job, football, and I could put my life in order. I started attending many courses, especially English language ones, as I was aiming to complete a Master's degree. During the English course, I fell in love. It was the first time that I had started to feel fulfilled in the UK. However, there was a problem. Due to unforeseen circumstances we had to get married quickly in order to stay together.

I knew that I was hurrying and breaking one of my rules of living with a person for at least a year before getting seriously committed, but I had to listen to my heart and take a bold decision. While we had great fun and genuinely loved each other, we had to live apart for over nine months and see each other only at the weekends as she was doing a postgraduate in music and I was living on the Surrey campus studying for my Master's degree.

When we moved in together I had to borrow money to pay the house deposit. We planned on renting out one of the rooms in the house, so my younger brother lived with us. In 2000 my father was killed in a horrific work accident, but I could not go to his funeral, as I had not finished my military service and they were legal issues.

Within one year of staying with my now ex-wife, I realized that we were going in different directions. There were too many demands and expectations imposed on me that did not allow me to flourish and follow my purpose, which led to our divorce.

All of this took a big toll on my health. I lost about 10 kg, my hair got thinner; I had ridges on my nails, and my digestion was a mess. I had eczema on my left leg, and had to have a knee arthroscopy after postponing it for years because of work. I was, in general, very confused, sad, lonely and feeling guilty, as I was the one who initiated the separation.

The question was now: What next? I decided to read as much as I could about relationships and health, as I could not work because of the knee arthroscopy I had. That experience made me realize that we always have responsibility for whatever is happening in our lives, whether it is good or bad. I also realized that I needed to be a bit selfish and look after my own health, career and passions.

Within two months I managed to find a job running high-end events at Claridge's Hotel, which was great for my career development and putting my life back on track. Because I enjoyed my job, being on my own and travelling to other countries, I found my wife, Svetlana. We have been together for twelve years, and are a happy and healthy family with two young kids, Odysseas and Athina.

While I was looking to solve my health problems I realized that there is lots of missing information when it comes to rebuilding health and recharging energy. It was obvious that a holistic approach is needed that looks much more at health stressors rather than just nutrition and training. It's vital to discover and resolve the root cause of a problem.

I may not be at the end of my journey, but now I am fully aligned with my life purpose and I live in gratitude and appreciation counting the blessings that I have in my life, helping others to rebuilt their health and recharge their energy whilst focusing on solutions rather than problems.

During my journey I have learned four key principles.

1. Make health the most important priority in your life. Unless you are healthy you cannot help the people around you and eventually your job/business, your relationships and your life will suffer as a consequence. "The one who has health

has hope and the one who has hope has everything." ~ Arab Proverb

2. Stop judging, comparing and controlling. This is a recipe for disaster, as you have no control over others.

3. Focus on the present. You cannot change the past, nor control the future. Most importantly, be very careful with the information that you listen to and the people you associate with. "Your thoughts become words, your words actions, your actions habits, your habits character and your character becomes destiny..." ~ Lao-Tzu

4. Change your understanding of the world. Nothing can harm you. You are a source energy and you will return to it. "Energy changes form, it never dies." Everything that happens in your life is perfect and is part of our personal and planetary evolution. "Within a disaster there is a seed for further grow" ~ Unknown

Miriam Hoolahan

Miriam Hoolahan is the owner of AppleCrisp Marketing – a marketing consultancy firm based in Vancouver, Canada. Prior to starting AppleCrisp in 2009, Miriam worked with a Toronto-based Fortune 500 Company in the industrial sector and for three of the leading banks in the U.K.

AppleCrisp works with global clients across a range of industries, specializing in market research and strategy. Miriam works closely with clients so they can unlock new market insights that will improve their relationships with customers. In 2013, Miriam made the move to Vancouver with her husband Richard, and loves the West Coast way of life and the natural beauty that surrounds her.

✉ **miriam@myapplecrisp.com**
🐦 **@AppleCrispMktg**

CHAPTER 12

DESERTED TO DELECTABLE: ARE YOU READY TO IGNITE YOUR SPARK?

By Miriam Hoolahan

Deserted. About five years ago, that's what I was. After moving across the Atlantic to the UK from my home country of Canada in 2006, I found myself in a very uneasy position. My marriage was ending, my work permit was now invalid and I was left without a job in a career I adored.

Not being able to practice my career was probably the hardest part of all. Although I struggled to find love for many years, success in my career was a constant. Immediately after finishing university in 2001, I started working for a Fortune 500 company in marketing. I was given great responsibility and got to travel around the world preaching my marketing gospel. I was doing work and launching brands in the first couple of years of my career that many marketing professionals never get to do at all. In 2006, all of a sudden that was gone, and I – frankly – was lost.

Throughout my life, there had always been a series of ups and downs – things never felt extremely easy. Money seemed to be at the center of much of this unease. Although I had been fortunate to grow up in a loving family, I always hoped things would be simpler. So, after meeting my first love and finding a career I enjoyed in the UK, I really did believe that life was on the up. Then, there I was at the end of 2009 – jobless, loveless and – pretty much – homeless.

After leaving the UK, I made my way back to my hometown Toronto in search of a job. But finding a job at the height of the recession was not an easy feat. After two months of sending out resumes, telling interviewers how great I was and trying to convince these same people I wasn't overqualified, I decided that I'd had enough. I had always aspired to start my own business and realized the time was now. Yes, part of me was hesitant – I always felt that I would start a business when my life was on a high, not out of survival. But I felt in my heart that the world was sending me a sign to take control of my life and destiny.

So, I did what many new entrepreneurs do: I sat down and thought of what I could offer clients in a unique way. I created what I believed was a good starting point and started to spread the word to everyone I knew – friends, family, ex-colleagues and whoever else would listen. Some were interested and some clearly thought I was crazy. Looking back to those first few weeks in Canada, I don't know how I got through the challenging questions and oddball stares – but I did. I still felt somewhat lost and wasn't convinced Toronto was where the magic would happen. Listening to my gut again I chatted with an old friend who also had a small business and she convinced me to take a bit of time to visit her – in Israel.

I booked a ticket and headed across the world. At first, it was great to catch up with my friend and to take in the beauty around me. I have always enjoyed Middle Eastern culture – the food, the music, their zest for living in the moment. However, after a couple of weeks, I started to think more and more about my new business. It started off well; I was working with clients I had met in my corporate days. However, these were short-term projects that I knew would dry up soon. Nervousness set in and like many "solopreneurs", I was wondering where the next paycheck would come from. As soon as these feelings surfaced, many other emotions came along too – not only about work but also about my personal life.

I realized after some long walks on the beach that I hadn't properly healed. I needed more time to focus on where my life had taken me and how I truly felt about it. However, in this world filled with bills to pay, how are you supposed to free your mind and deal with some of these real emotions? I'd just started a new business and desperately wanted it to succeed. Thinking up a different solution was what I needed – I just knew it.

Starting to think of creative ideas, I realized that I was in a unique situation being in Israel. I looked into volunteering on a kibbutz, working part of the day for my shelter and food. A kibbutz works like a tiny community, where residents share tasks around the neighborhood, contributing to daily life in exchange for living expenses. There are many of these communities scattered around the country, and it is a unique and relatively peaceful way to live. I knew that volunteering in this way wouldn't be glamorous and I had no idea what to expect. But, again, my gut told me it was worth a try.

I was placed at a kibbutz in the south, right in the middle of the desert – with almost nothing around but sand and sky. For a girl who grew up in the city, this was a definite change of scenery. Being dumped in the desert – so to speak – was exactly what I needed. I didn't need to worry about money since all my food and shelter was covered by the few hours of volunteering I did every day. The remaining hours I could spend working on selective projects or thinking about my vision for AppleCrisp Marketing.

Through the desert I found my center. By giving myself the space to search inside without everyday stresses, I realized that the key to my happiness was in helping others. Even though AppleCrisp wouldn't cure world hunger, I knew that I could make my own mark.

During my few months of exploration in the desert, I also revived my love of running. Just as the sun was setting, I would put on my running shoes and head along a trail around the perimeter of the kibbutz. There were nights where there was nothing in sight except for the stars. At times, I would actually run with my eyes shut as I listened to some of my most beloved music. I can just picture it now. My thoughts would run from good memories of the past, to how I felt in the present to hopes and dreams for my future. The feeling of being so free and truly feeling like I knew who I was again helped me feel complete.

There were days where I pondered staying and making a life in the desert. Many may think that subscribing to a life like this is crazy and unrealistic. However, many do indeed choose this, and I completely understand why. Listening to my gut once again, I decided that I wasn't a desert dweller and after three months of desert life, I headed back to the city. However, I came out of the desert feeling like a new person – a woman who had ignited her spark for life, love and helping others.

Since this special time in my life, I've been thrown some curve balls that have caused me to feel challenged. I catch myself thinking back to those nights in the desert where over a period of months I went from feeling deserted to delectable. I close my eyes sometimes and think about running in the beauty of the desert stars. This reminds me of what I want in my life, why sometimes we need to endure failures or challenges in order to realize our resilience.

Failure is actually a gift to us all – the gift of challenge and an opportunity for learning. Since my time in the desert, I've learned that it takes a few simple steps to turn setbacks into the fuel that can ignite the spark within you. In my life, I try to:

1. Embrace uncertainty & listen to my gut when challenges arise.

2. Understand that everyone has a different path, so it's important to do what's right for me – regardless of what others say.

3. Remember my center – a memory of running in the desert is mine, what about you?

4. When life throws me a lime, I try my best to make a margarita.

I truly believe that without my romp in the desert, I wouldn't be where I am today. After coming from a place of feeling fizzled and deflated, it ignited my spark for what I wanted in life and reminded me of my hopes, dreams and desires. Those three months of being deserted taught me a lot about myself and turned my life into one that is truly delectable. Are you ready to experience the same and ignite your own spark?

Tom Evans

Tom Evans is a broadcast TV engineer turned author's mentor turned channel, healer and mystic. Tom's books take the esoteric and make it exoteric. That is, his aim is to transform the unknown and hidden into the known and understood.

As an engineer, he has an amazing understanding of the physical sciences. As a student of both Eastern and Western mysticism, he has an insight into the metaphysical landscape. Like all humans, he is a conduit from the above to the below.

Tom's passion is to help people find their soul path and to take control over their own evolution.

www.tomevans.co

f **facebook.com/thebookwright**

𝕏 **twitter.com/thebookwright**

CHAPTER 13

THE ART OF STRESSLESS SUCCESS

By Tom Evans

In the 1960s, a teacher in a primary school was casting the annual nativity play. She used both logic and fairness in making her choices for the parts. Joseph had the most lines to say, so the teacher chose the boy who had the highest marks in last summer's tests. Of course, she didn't check if he could actually act.

When it came to rehearsals, it became clear very quickly that the boy was a quivering wreck, and she'd put far too much on his small shoulders. She chose another boy and asked the first boy to play the part of an innkeeper. "There's no room at the inn," was all the boy needed to say, and only once.

Even this small task proved too much and the boy eventually found a comfortable position in the play as an angel on the back row of the chorus without any wings. All he had to do was mouth the words and pretend he was singing.

When the boy started his career, the mere suggestion of getting him to perform or speak in public would send him into a blind panic. Eventually he succumbed, as his job needed him to share his experience and wisdom. He slowly mastered the art of presenting but always preferred to play second fiddle and share the stage with someone else taking the lead and introducing him.

The boy had become quite a driven young man and was well known and well respected in his industry as an innovator and visionary. By the time he was 40, he'd built two hi-tech businesses and achieved quite an amount of commercial success. His peers looked at him as someone who had made it. He had a beautiful wife, a very nice house in the country and all the chattels anyone could wish for. The success though had come at a price.

The first business he had steered through the recession of the 1990s, and the second business survived the Dot Com boom and bust. In his mid-40's, he was pretty frazzled by it all and walked away from the second business without a job to go to. All through his life, he'd landed on his feet and slid from one opportunity to another without so much as a job interview.

Inside, he felt he was a failure and questioned the point of everything. He then began to make a reasonable living as an IT subcontractor. He limped from contract to contract, just earning enough money to do anything he wanted to do. He still had the beautiful wife he'd met in his 20s and the nice house in the country. But he was bored.

In frustration he booked a session with a life coach who said something that really hit home. She said, "Do you want to live your life in splendid mediocrity?" She quickly diagnosed that each time he'd become financially successful; he'd also become really stressed. As a result, he'd now become pretty adept at avoiding success. She taught him how to meditate to help with the stress, while also giving him some pointers on how to redefine success.

It got him thinking or, more specifically, not-thinking. After a few months of meditation, some weird things started to happen that resulted in him making an unexpected career twist. He wrote a book by accident. In fact, he found out later that he channeled it, but had no idea what channeling was at the time.

The book took off and people admired what he'd done and asked if he could help them could write a book too. As a helpful chap, he obliged. Before he knew it, he'd become an author's mentor.

Quite a few of his clients seemed to suffer from writer's block and he had no tools with which to help them, so he did some training in hypnotherapy and regression. Pretty quickly he found he could clear virtually any blockage of the creative flow. He also learned how to connect people with their guides or Creative Muse.

What's more, each case of writer's block really turned out to be a life block. Not only did he help people get their books published, but also he helped them get their lives back on the straight and narrow.

Being enterprising, he even wrote some books on the very subject of clearing creative blocks and how we can tune into ideas and make them actually happen. This led to his bête noire surfacing once more. As an author and so-called expert, people invited him to be interviewed on podcasts and talk about these subjects on stage. He was initially petrified at the prospect.

Starting with small audiences, he found his voice. He'd even run workshops for up to 40 people or so. Slowly but surely, the audiences got bigger and he found he was OK so long as the audience was appreciative and receptive. It wasn't long before the demons that had lived with him for 40 years were vanquished. It was only in his 50s, when he began to actually get paid for speaking that he recalled the incident of the nativity play.

While he felt pretty cool that he was over that hurdle, a bigger and deeper issue started to come to the surface.

Now he'd started to become known and recognized in his new field, he craved the recognition that he perceived some of his peers seemed to have gained. He was liked and respected within relatively small circles but, when it came to national and certainly international recognition, success as this new author persona eluded him.

With some internalizing and reflection, the nub of the issue dawned on the man. By redefining success, he could become an instant success. His nice house in the country meant that he lived cheek by jowl with some pretty successful people. They were earning a pretty packet. They had a daily commute to a job in The City, a wife who stayed at home and children at public school. Some of them turned out to be pretty stressed too and not at all happy with their lot.

The man realized his commute took one minute and he basically did what he liked when he liked, which would be bliss to many. Real success was only a matter actually achieving redefined level of success without the associated stress.

You may of course have guessed who this man is by now.

Now in my mid-50s, I can look back on my life and audit how far I have really come. Unlike many, I've had a pretty easy life. I haven't had to come back from the edge or suffered any life-threatening trauma. I have been in a stable, enriching and fulfilling relationship for over 30 years, which blossoms and deepens year on year. Each year I am creating better and better work, and my portfolio is now quite substantial.

The main lesson I have learned is that it's natural for us to strive for something better and to measure ourselves against others. When we use others as a benchmark, however, any successes that we have achieved can easily seem paltry.

By stretching ourselves little by little and slowly putting our head above the parapet, something amazing happens. Firstly we find that people, in general, aren't out to get us. Secondly, we find we are capable of things we could never dream of.

While I wouldn't necessarily put myself forward for a part in an amateur play, I have no fear of public speaking these days. I don't get complacent and take any talk lightly though and continually find ways to improve.

With each book I write, I explore new themes and challenge myself to become a better writer. I started writing what were essentially workshop manuals. Nowadays I've channeled works of pure philosophy, and shortly will embark on works of complete fiction.

Before taking on a whole novel, I've taken yet another small step and written a book of short stories.

Telling my story of how a shy boy, turned businessman, turned author is not meant to be a showcase for my talents. There is a much bigger learning to be shared. By realizing what blocks are holding us back, which are often seeded in our childhood, and overcoming them, new doors will always open for us. By taking on new learnings, even bigger opportunities for growth come our way.

Being asked to write this very chapter has lead me to a bigger realization. Do I make loads of money from my writing and my new, unexpected career you may ask? The answer is unequivocally not. I have never earned so little money in my whole career, but there are some upsides, which are incalculable.

I am really content. Priceless.

I can heal with touch and a thought. Priceless.

I can channel Universal Wisdom and teach others how to do it. Priceless.

I can bend and stretch the fabric of time to get more done in less hours. Priceless.

So am I successful? Yes!

Am I resting on my laurels? No!

My new mantra is this. You can only take one thing with you – your evolution – and you can only leave one thing behind, and that's your art.

DJ Sobanjo

DJ Sobanjo is a leading personal and leadership development expert, author, speaker, coach and consultant. He has been engaging, inspiring and developing people across the world for over 10 years.

He is driven by a mission to teach, train, inspire and motivate everyone who comes in touch with him to live more productive and effective lives.

His core message is "Maximized Living," which is about being the best person, business or organization you could possibly be. He delivers result-oriented programs in the areas of tactical people skills, leadership skills, sales and marketing skills and strategic personal and business growth.

CHAPTER 14

THANKS FOR BEING A DIFFERENCE MAKER

By DJ Sobanjo

"Our MD has taken a liking to you," Muna, the HR director said as we walked back to the lift. This was my final day, and I was flying back to London in a few hours, so I was saying my goodbyes to some of the wonderful people I had met in the short period I'd been here.

It had been a wonderful experience for me and I had already begun to see changes happen within the bank, but I was especially pleased that the Managing Director & HR Director were impressed.

The taxi had arrived to take me to the airport and my bags were loaded into the vehicle. Muna was there to see me off, and just before I boarded, I turned to say a final goodbye and stretched out my hand, but she hugged me and said, "Thanks for being a difference maker." For a moment I froze as her statement sunk in, but I quickly recovered, said thanks, then hopped into the taxi.

As we drove through the streets of the beautiful city of Gaborone, Muna's words kept replaying in my head: "Thanks for being a difference maker."

Here's the story.

It was a cold winter morning in 2001, and I was sitting in my pastor's office. You see, I'd only just migrated to England a few weeks before, and having recently joined the church, I felt it was right to get to meet my pastor and make myself accountable to him – hence the visit.

I can't remember most of what was said that morning, but one thing I do remember vividly was looking at my pastor and saying, "I'm not here in England to chase the Pound, I'm here to be a difference maker." I meant what I said but little did I know what was in store for me.

I had a strong passion to help people be more productive and effective, and a strong desire to build a career doing that. However, my first goal was to get a job. I'd recently gotten married to my wonderful wife, Buki, and the plan was to get a job so she could come over from Nigeria and we could start to build our family together. I really didn't think that was going to be a problem.

Even now, almost 14 years later, I can't hold back the tears as I remember those trying times. I went to my local job center in Woolwich, South East London, quite confident that if I put myself forward for a couple of management positions, I would get a few interview invites and then land my first job. How wrong I was.

I applied for 23 management positions that first day, within a couple of days I received 23 rejection letters in the post. I hate rejection; nothing knocks self-esteem and your sense of self-worth like rejection. I was knocked back, but I concluded that if I wasn't good enough for management positions, I should apply for assistant management positions. So I went back to the job center, this time applied for over 20 assistant manager roles and guess what? Yes, I was rejected for those roles too.

I took another step down and started to apply for supervisory roles. No luck at all.

At this point it seemed like all my dreams were literally falling apart before my very eyes. It wasn't meant to be like this. But it only got worse.

Now I was desperate for work. I needed money and things looked very bleak. I was ready to do anything as long as I'd get paid and it wasn't against the law or my core values. I went back to the job center, this time I was looking at everything, all those jobs I had passed over initially were now all attractive to me, anything – security guard, factory hand, you name it – as long as they'd pay me, I was ready to do it.

I applied for over 50 roles that day and only got 2 interviews. I remember sitting down one afternoon after going through a hoard of rejection letters. At this point my confidence was completely sapped. I sat there and I cried; then I prayed and God must have heard me because a couple of hours later a friend came over and told me London Underground was recruiting station assistants. A few weeks before I would have refused to apply for this role, but hey, this job was a lot better than a factory hand, and I couldn't even get an interview for that role, so I applied.

To cut a long story short, I applied for the role, got an interview and I landed the job. I'm sure at the time I must have been the most excited station assistant in the whole of London. It was during my induction that I first came across the Corporate Trainer role and really loved it. I was advised to get out of station operations and move into a white-collar role in the organization if I desired to work as a corporate trainer, and that became my next challenge.

Every week I would browse the internal vacancy pack, look for jobs I felt I was qualified for and complete application forms. "Oh DJ, stop wasting your time" many of my colleagues would say. "Why don't you just follow the traditional route to operational management and forget this pipe dream?"

In my first year I must have received at least 60 rejection letters for various internal jobs I applied for. Finally, I decided to listen to the voice of reason, and I applied for the role of station supervisor. It was during my station supervisor training that I discovered what I really wanted to do. We went through a management development course and sitting in the training room, I just saw myself doing that. I knew I was so far away from it and had experienced lots of disappointments in my career thus far, but I really believed this was my future.

I began to picture myself training and coaching managers and leaders, not just in my company, but also across the world. I bought books, courses and literally threw myself into anything to do with management & leadership development. My colleagues at work thought I was nuts.

During that period various trainer roles were advertised, and I applied believing it would be easier for me to cross from a trainer role to management development when the opportunities came, but I was continually getting rejected. Nevertheless, I refused to give up on my dream. I was going to be a difference maker and management development was going to be my vehicle for achieving that.

I can still remember that afternoon. It was December 2005 when I saw a management development trainer vacancy. I must admit I was a little scared with all the previous rejections flashed across my mind. I said a quick prayer and applied for it. I was invited for an interview told a few colleagues, to which one replied, "DJ, don't waste your time. They don't give these jobs to station staff like you. You're just there to make up the numbers." Well I chose to ignore him and landed the job.

That was the beginning of the turnaround for me. That job gave me the opportunity to do what I love, and it created the enabling environment for me to become great at it. This was not just a job for me; it was my passion, and I was getting paid to do what I loved.

After working with the company for 6 years, I decided to leave and start my own consultancy. This opened up new opportunities for me across the world, including a project with a major bank in Africa.

Muna's words were echoing in my ears: "Thanks for being a difference maker."

Yes, it was a tough, challenging experience and I almost gave up, but I didn't. When I look back at my life, what I went through and where I am now, it was well worth it. I'm glad that now, in my own small way, I'm living my dream of being a difference maker.

CoachKemi

CoachKemi, CEO & Founder of How2Think is a Personal Development Trainer, Seminar Leader, NLP Practitioner and Thought-Coach, Youth Worker & Inspirational Speaker who helps fraught, frustrated & fed up female entrepreneurs who seem unable to increase their profits discover Grade A thoughts that will make them more money, enabling them to live a life of abundance.

She also supports young people between the ages of 16 and 25 who are struggling with the challenges of completing their education while running a business or working, as well as those who lack financial education and are unsure of their purpose.

CHAPTER 15

A LIFE LESS NORMAL
By CoachKemi

What a life it has been.

I watch my Self live. Yes, I am one of those humans, catching up with my life after I have lived it, as if I was not the one who lived. I got married when I was 26 years old, had two children by the time I was 30 and separated from my husband when I was 42, consequently divorcing him when I was 46 years old.

But my life started at 42. I came out of the shadows; I came into the real world.

Where I had to survive OR thrive. Where I had to survive AND thrive. Where I had to live or die. Where I had to know what I thought I knew, all over again. Where I had to meet ME for the first time ever. Where I finally realized that success and failure are real. I choose. I cannot have both. Where I had to decide whether I wanted to make it in life and if it were actually possible to do so.

Oh, what a journey.

I was not a businessperson by any means. The only way I could describe myself up until age 42 was a woman who would not allow her gender to stop her from being or doing anything, as long as it was good or if it would help someone else.

I desired to be on the stages of the world. I wanted to go out there to help people. I wanted to be known as the go-to person for "stick-to-itiveness," the "you-can-make-it-come-what-may" woman, the "bounce back" woman. But I was a far cry from that.

I was one of those who wore her heart on her sleeve. Everything was painful; everything was to be reacted to. Everyone had to understand how I felt and was feeling, and I mean, *everyone*.

Yes, I'm sure you're thinking: "42!?! You were 42 years old before you began to grow up?" Yes! I was.

You see, I did not know I was 42 by then. All I knew was that a year ends, another begins. I simply carry on. Everyone around me seemed to be more important than I was, so I would stop my life just to ensure they were ok and then go back to wearing my heart on my sleeve when *they* would not reach out to me.

But, at 42, separation forced me into becoming a wiser woman. By then, I had been married for sixteen and a half years and did not know it until the separation happened.

It was so painful. I thought I would not make it. I ended up a single parent with two children. I was not that kind of person. I fought for my marriage and would have fought some more if not for the fact that my life seemed to be ebbing away. It was not getting better, even though I was a Christian and sure knew how to pray.

I remember when he left. My daughter was in her first teenage year and my son was on his way into his. For 2 weeks I would get some food and watch soap operas until I had to go pick them up from school. You see, their father and I had agreed that I would stay at home once we began to have children. I did, and I enjoyed it.

However, I did not enjoy the near-poverty existence that we had. I never travelled anywhere, but that was okay because I was able to keep wearing the same clothes for years and years. We had to move house once he left because the bailiffs were coming. We moved down the road and lived there for 5 years until we were evicted.

I was intent on starting a coaching business. I qualified as a Gold Coach and NLP Practitioner as my cure for the emotional ailments of being separated. It worked. The almost yearlong course took me places in my mind I had never been to and introduced me to myself all over again. I was liberated. I knew God so much better, and I was more secure.

However, I knew next to nothing about starting a business. But I went for it anyway. Lack of money was a huge, issue, but I did not let it stop me – until I stopped.

One day, after my husband left, I asked God, "Why do we behave the way we do? Why do we, with all of the good things we know and should do, why do we still go off the track and mess things up on a really grand scale?"

He answered, "Because of the way you think."

I looked for the word "think" in the Bible and found Proverbs chapter 23, verse 7. Go read it. We are what we think; we become what we think; we will always be what we think.

So that became my mission. I thought it would work like magic.

It didn't.

I obtained a second degree in youth and community work, as working with young people is another passion of mine. In between all of these, I had two growing teenagers to bring up by myself. Those were harrowing years. But somehow, by the Grace of God, I stayed sane.

Here's what I learned: I have to take responsibility for my thoughts, my thought-life. It is a continuous learning experience. I am a result of the thoughts I have harbored and allowed to course through my mind. I have no one else to blame, not even the devil. I wasn't attaining or achieving those great things I could see in my mind's eye because of *me*.

While researching separated/divorced women, here's what I found: if she has a job, she will eventually lose it, become an addict, become overweight and if she has children, may eventually lose her children to the state. I flung the newspaper I was reading away from me as if it stank and stood up defiantly, saying out loud, "THIS WILL NEVER HAPPEN TO ME!" I was scared.

But it did. Everything happened to me. I was admitted to hospital suffering from exhaustion. Both my children went through harrowing and unrepeatable crises, one after another.

I had to grow up when I realized that no one was going to help me, but me. Not even God. He, after all, has done all there is to do.

What was left was for me to take that walk to the edge of the cliff and step over knowing that I would be caught just before I hit the ground. Then get up and begin to walk ahead intentionally with raw determination, deliberately and purposefully, armed with large doses of courage, confidence and boldness with the words, "I CAN! I CAN! I CAN!" erupting from my mouth.

Today, I am fit, strong, able and stable. I am at peace and I refuse to give up. After all, the answer lies within me. It is with me what I choose to become and what I choose to do with what I know.

Today, I am *the* CoachKemi – a mother and grandmother who is also a qualified youth worker, helping female entrepreneurs and speaking in universities and churches to young people.

Changing your thoughts and knowing how to think will change your life, only if you want to.

Now, GO DO!

Sheila Kadeer

Known as the Fairy Godmother of Magical Transformations, Sheila is a Female Empowerment Coach working with women with wounded hearts from domestic violence or trauma. In her own unique way she guides women to become warrior goddesses in love, life and business.

Her vision is that the business model moves from the old masculine paradigm to a workplace filled with confident female leaders able to fully express their divine feminine without fear or consequence. She runs a coaching practice called Cinderella Executive Coaching where her clients can heal, clear limiting beliefs and blocks and create a positive powerful future.

www.cinderellaexecutivecoaching.com

📞 **Phone: +44 (0)7803 956523**

Ⓢ **Skype: sheila.kadeer**

✉ **Email: sheila.kadeer@gmail.com**

f **Facebook: The Fairy Godmother of Magical Transformations**

🐦 **Twitter: @InnerMagicCoach**

CHAPTER 16

FROM WOUNDED HEART TO WARRIOR GODDESS

By Sheila Kadeer

My name is Sheila Kadeer and my life has been a long journey of pain and recovery. Going to the depths of despair and wondering if I would ever get to be happy, thinking I did not deserve to be happy. Trapped in a dark place with no one to talk to. Feeling small and vulnerable. Longing to reach out to someone but scared of the repercussions. Putting on a mask to go to work and pretending I had it all, portraying a woman that was so together and dedicated to her job.

Trying to work my way up the long and hard corporate ladder. But when I stepped out of the office, my knees would tremble, I would feel sick, I did not want to go home. Home was a place of misery, punishment and hurt. I wanted a happy home and I tried so hard to make it a home, but nothing I could ever do would be good enough. No matter how hard I tried, I would never be able to get it right.

When I look at my life now, it is so different. I have been on a long path of self-discovery, and I have healed my wounded heart and all the pain within it. It took time, but I am strong now. I am strong for myself and more importantly for other women, too. I do not want other women to fear going home like I once did. Home should be a safe place. Your home should be your sanctuary.

I was a wounded heart for many many years. All my relationships were abusive; my life was hard. Everything I did was a struggle both at work and in love – or what I thought was love.

I was a very quiet and shy person. Introverted with an open heart, wanting to please everyone, wanting to be accepted. I was always an outsider it seemed. I did not have a large circle of friends; I preferred my own company and the company of animals. I was academic and continued to add to my skills while working in the corporate sector. I worked hard but never got the breaks I felt I deserved.

Out at my local club in 1994 I met the man that changed my life. He was dressed smartly and as I looked at him, I felt safe. He dropped me home, and as I tried to let him out, my front door jammed and he was locked in. He could not leave, so we talked and talked. I felt so in tune with him.

We began dating. He treated me like a princess. I felt blessed to have found the man I thought I would marry. I had my own house and he moved in within months. We tried for a baby and very quickly I fell pregnant. We were overjoyed, but something was not right. He changed. Gone was the loving man who worshipped me. He became verbally abusive and extremely jealous.

I was late home from an evening out with college friends and when I got in he was not there. He was hiding in a cupboard. He started accusing me of seeing someone else, swearing and throwing things at me. His behavior became steadily worse. I told no one, I held down a good job and kept strong; he made me believe it was my fault. He was drinking heavily too, although I did not know that at the beginning.

At a few months pregnant, he held a knife to my throat and threatened to cut the baby out of my stomach. He pushed an ironing board into my stomach while I was pregnant because I asked where he had been. After my daughter was born, the violence carried on and escalated in severity. I lost count of the violent episodes and many took place in front of her. I would be punched, kicked and my food spat in.

I tried so many times to end the relationship, but he threatened to take my daughter away from me and I believed him. People just don't realize what goes on behind closed doors. They say, "Well you should have just left!" It's not that easy, I can assure you. You have no self-esteem, your spirit is broken, and you have been alienated from friends and family. If you do try and leave, then you know you may lose your life. He had threatened to kill me if I did, and I believed him.

He used to keep a baseball bat in his car as protection, but one day he brought the bat and hid it in a cupboard. I was getting close to finding out he was having an affair and when I confronted him about it, he went for the baseball bat. This was premeditated as he had also locked the back doors so I could not get out. He took that bat to me while my daughter screamed hiding under a table. He wanted to kill me.

Somehow I got out of the house. I must have had a guardian angel looking over me, as I came out with only minor injury. He was arrested for attempted murder and was such a smooth talker that he got away with it. He was released with no charge, so he could come back to the house. The police were not as hot on domestic violence back then as they are today.

I began a civil court case for custody of my daughter, and, as expected, he played dirty the whole way through. He lied and lied, and he was good at it. I was devoid of emotion in court. I was all cried out, which was to my detriment because a judge ruled that he would have interim custody and live in the house I was paying for while I moved out and had contact twice a week. What the hell!

I cried a bucket load of tears that night, and to see the fear on my daughter's face will haunt me forever. This was my lowest point, and I knew I had failed – failed as a mother, as I could not protect her from him, failed by the system that should have been protecting me.

At this point my warrior goddess woke up and took over. I reconnected to spirit and started to listen to their guidance. I began to work with my angels; after all, I believe they stepped in when he wanted to kill me with the bat. I didn't discount using a bit of earthly help too.

I employed a private detective to prove he was lying, and finally I had the evidence I needed for court. He had moved his 17-year-old girlfriend into our home after promising the court that he would not have her around our daughter. In court, our neighbors and add his in front of ex-girlfriend all gave evidence in my favor. I used positive thought and envisioned the final outcome. I prayed to the universe each night to ask that I win the court case. I invited angels into the courtroom to aid my communication. I asked Archangel Raphael to help communicate the truth. I watched in awe as his barrister could not speak when directing the court after Archangel Raphael was asked to reside. My evidence was given easily, and I watched him tie himself in knots when talking to the judge. Finally, I won and was awarded costs because he was proven to be acting maliciously.

I had my daughter back, but still things were not quite over. She needed trauma therapy. I saw pictures she had drawn of when asked about her dad. She drew in black a picture of her with rain falling over her, and she drew a picture in color of me on a rainbow colored unicorn. When the child psychologist asked her about the picture, she said, "I dreamt that Mummy would come to save me on a rainbow unicorn." Heartbreaking.

I knew at that moment that this was meant to happen. That rainbow unicorn is my guiding influence. I know I am here to help other women who have experienced pain and trauma through domestic violence. Without the experience and the bruises to my body and my heart, I would not be the spiritually connected warrior goddess I am today.

Pain is part of life, but we don't need to let that hold us back. I give thanks to him for the experience, as it has taught me that I am a strong woman and I can achieve anything no matter what life throws at me.

Domestic violence goes on behind closed doors. It doesn't have to be physical; it can be emotional, mental and financial. It is not acceptable, and there are agencies and support groups that can help. Decide when you want to step into your warrior goddess and seek out your own Fairy Godmother on the Rainbow Unicorn.

Jay K-Frederick

Jay K-Frederick is an award winning marketing and communications expert and speaker living in London with her husband and two cats, Sprinkle and Champagne.

In 2014, she founded B.O.L.D. Living – a platform that encourages women to live boldly irrespective of their life's journey, by using their power story.

She has worked with Reuters and photographic journalist Chiara Ceolin to produce a short documentary about female genital cutting (FGC) that was empowering, thought provoking and insightful, as it challenged the status quo on labeling, and the use of disempowering terminology that increased stigma and shame. She has become a sought after speaker, speaking to government ministers, women in business and in secondary schools.

In 2013, fed up with perpetrators outshining the real heroes of sexual violence, she created Red Lipstick Day - The Movement, a powerful initiative to celebrate and empower women living with the effects of sexual violence.

www.jaykfrederick.com

✉ **jaykamarafrederick@gmail.com**

CHAPTER 17

THERE IS POWER AND PURPOSE IN YOUR STORY

By Jay K-Frederick

My name is Jay K-Frederick, a unique woman that not so uniquely loves the finer things in life. Disempowering terms annoy me and individuals who do not give themselves permission to embrace life make me cry. They are missing out on the greatest time of their life. Rest will come when it's time for me to go to heaven, but in the meantime, I have work to do, champagne to drink, family and friends to love and adventures to partake in.

I have been called many names – a victim, mutilated, ugly and stupid – terms that I reject, and I refuse to succumb to the negative role and connotations associated with them. I believe that our experiences make up the sum of who we are, and that one should be known more for their character than what they have been through in life. My aim is not to change the whole world, but to influence change one person at a time.

My life is full of stories, some sad and traumatic, others funny and dramatic. I see each story as a gift that keeps on giving. Not only have they shaped me, but they have also helped others.

Some parts of my journey I have detested; others, I have loved the pants off, but irrespective, I wouldn't change what I have been through because it has bought me here. It has given me insight and wisdom that I would have only picked up in books and it has given me awareness, passion and compassion, connected me spiritually and given my life a bit of spice. And when I wake up in the morning I say, "Thank you Lord! What would you have me do today? Show me how to be a better person and show me who needs a touch of you through me today."

Having cried a river, experienced loneliness, loss, immense sadness and pain, hate and a debilitating sense of shame and self hate, my desire is that no one experiences those things. This is the chapter of my life I have titled *The Wilderness Years*. None of this would be obvious to the casual observer or to my closest friends or family members; no one knew, and, to be fair, there was no interest on my part to share.

Reflecting back on my journey so far, my chest fills with pride because there has been no area in my life in which I have failed. What has unfolded has created many chapters that I can learn from. Let me explain.

The root word failure/fail in Latin is *delinquo* and *defectus* defined as, "be wanting to/ fail in duty, commit a crime." The English Oxford Dictionary defines failure as, "not doing something, lack of success, a person who is not successful." If there has been failure on my part, it has been withholding the knowledge, learning and opinions that I have acquired. Now I know I have the ability to change attitudes, influence change and potentially stop someone from going through the same thing as me

At times I have lost my way, lost my sense of self, lost a job, didn't make the grade on an exam, kissed the wrong guy, drank way to much, offended someone, gotten myself into debt, hurt my family and friends and failed in business. But by whose standards are those things failures? Are they not lessons of life, love and business from which we can grow?

If I took on board the failure as defined by the Oxford English Dictionary, I think I would have given up on my journey a long time ago. Now, that would have been a total demonstration of failure and a travesty. Instead, I redefined what success means to me and have made it my mission to be successful in being the person I have been created to be.

I have learned, not without stubbornness and struggle to let go of the labels and bad habits and surrender to my purpose. When you surrender, your struggle, no matter what that is will *have to* turn around. You see, nothing lasts and every day is a new opportunity to try again, but only when you surrender. That's why I love each day – rain, shine or snow – it's my change to start again.

That's why I say with confidence I haven't failed at much because I haven't given up. When I give up, stop desiring and pursing the things I desire then I have failed, and I can't do that because I have a life of purpose to live. Benjamin Button says it best, "Some people, were born to sit by a river. Some get struck by lightning. Some have an ear for music. Some are artists. Some swim. Some know buttons. Some know Shakespeare. Some are mothers. And some people, dance".

Me, I was born to inspire through my stories and influence change with my words. For a long time shame was my constant shadow, fear my companion and silence my solution. Now I am proud of whom I am because there is no shame in living to be a successful version of me. I have worked hard to gain the strength to galvanize my whole being from the top of my head to the soles of my feet to live, walk, talk, hustle, love, laugh and sing with purpose, and when I fall backwards I simply start again.

"For what it's worth: it's never too late or, in my case, too early to be whoever you want to be. There's no time limit, start whenever you want. You can change or stay the same; there are no rules to this thing. We can make the best or the worst of it. I hope you make the best of it. And I hope you see things that startle you. I hope you feel things you never felt before. I hope you meet people with a different point of view. I hope you live a life you're proud of. If you find that you're not, I hope you have the strength to start all over again." – Benjamin Button

There is nothing new under the sun. How I got through my challenges is not unique to me, but what is unique is my story. No one has lived it but me. Based on that, I make no apologies for my options because they have been informed by my journey. Likewise your story in love, business and life is the most powerful asset you have.

No one is created equal and neither are our stories. Don't be afraid to own yours. Be proud of it and most importantly to share it, especially with those younger than you. You are a vessel of wisdom and influence. You can give them hope and a new direction. Additionally, you never know the doors of opportunity that will open for you because "the real you" has shown up.

The most frequent question I am asked is when did I stop being a victim. It's a strange question to answer, as I have no memory of being one.

One has to be realistic about life, in that as long as you are breathing, there is a risk that you can be hurt. If a time like that occurs, I promise you will get through it and life will continue – if you want it to.

If you've been through a traumatic experience you will be in recovery for the rest of your life, but it doesn't mean you can't strive for greatness! On my journey I may have down days, occasionally get stuck in sinking sand, find myself in a valley or up on the highest mountain. The most important thing is that I never give up, because I have the right to be here, and a duty to share my story – not for my sake, but to help those that can be inspired not to give in to the what to what society calls "failure."

Give yourself permission to enjoy life, whatever that looks like to you. For me that is having a full time spiritual practice, which has been my lifeline, daily forgiving myself and others, express gratitude and love.

Go for walks in all types of weather, it's beautiful to feel nature around you. Look up into the sky, you may be fortunate to see a messages in the clouds just for you. Have an open heart to be a blessing and be blessed, be determined to live your best day daily. But most importantly, know that you are loved deeply and that you are not alone. And lastly, remember the day you give up is the day you fail!

Julie Barnes

My name is Julie Barnes. I'm a certified life coach, Huffington Post blogger, inspirational speaker, the founder of Julie Barnes Live and a bit of a Betty Badass.

My mission is to inspire, transform and celebrate women throughout the world to be more, to follow passions, to overcome fears, and to take all the dreams lovingly written down over the years in journals and bring them to reality. To live without regret and to kick off the self-induced shackles that keep so many women prisoners in a life of contentment. If I can do it, so can you!

www.juliebarneslive.com

CHAPTER 18

3 KEYS TO LIVING FEARLESSLY

By Julie Barnes

Have you ever thought how it would feel to live your life fearlessly?

To be able to kick off the self-induced shackles that keep so many people prisoners in a life of contentment while they secretly long for more. If only it weren't for fear of... you fill in the blank.

If you were to ask the average person why they haven't reached an important goal yet, you're bound to hear a fear of some kind in their answer: fear of failure, fear of what people will think, or even fear of success. It's these fears that stop so many people from taking the required action to reach their dreams.

I was once one of those people. I had notebooks full of ideas, notes and dreams that I had lovingly written down over the years, things I would one day do. But just the mere thought of taking action to make any one of them happen would bring up my fears.

That all changed after I experienced something both devastating and life-changing; it was the beginning of my journey to living life fearlessly.

It wasn't an easy journey. I learned that living life fearlessly doesn't happen overnight. It takes a lot perseverance and tenacity.

I also learned there are three keys necessary to live life fearlessly.

1. The strength to let go of being a victim and move beyond your life circumstances.
2. The courage to live your dreams.
3. The continued commitment to invest in yourself.

My life circumstances made it easy for me to see myself as a victim, but I realized that I had a choice to make. I could either stay stuck in despair, or I could let go of being a victim and move beyond my life circumstances.

FINDING THE STRENGTH TO LET GO

We are all dealt a particular hand in life; it's how we choose to play that hand that affects the outcome. We like to blame our stories for where we are in our lives. It's when we choose to rise above our stories and take our power back that life begins to change.

My life hasn't always been a bed of roses. It's been a life full of pivotal events that could make a Lifetime movie.

I had a typical childhood until fourth grade. Then the first pivotal event happened: a period of sexual abuse began that lasted about two years. The shame I carried from the abuse took a toll on my self-worth well into my adult years.

It also significantly affected the choices I made in life. One of those choices was just to go through the motions in life and hide out. It wasn't until I reflected back on my life that I was amazed at the continuous effort I subconsciously took to protect myself from being seen in the world.

I chose my initial career based on the fact that I could continue to hide. For about 15 years, I worked in various accounting positions. I worked with numbers, not people. It was the perfect place to be invisible.

Even while hiding out, I knew there had to be more to life. I still had dreams. Becoming an entrepreneur was one of those dreams, but I let fear stop me. I thought I didn't know enough to start a business, and I didn't have the correct letters behind my name.

But every morning on my drive to work, my stomach ached. The closer I got to the office, the worse it became, just at the mere thought of sitting in a cubicle for another eight hours of my life.

I started researching how I could use the skills I did have to start a business. That's when I discovered virtual assisting. I thought, *How cool*. I could work from anywhere. It would also allow me to travel with my husband, Ron, a natural gas pipeline welder. I immediately took action to become a certified virtual assistant. I launched my website, found some clients, and suddenly I was an entrepreneur. I had reached one of my dreams.

But then, the most devastating thing happened. In 2008, my son, Chris, took his life. I knew that this was a direct result of his addiction to oxycodone. His doctor had prescribed the drug for his back pain two years earlier. Before that, Chris was a good kid. Watching him transform into an addict that ultimately took his life broke my heart open.

It also brought up my past sexual abuse that I'd never dealt with. I spent the next couple of years in a ball of sadness. I felt like a zombie walking through life.

In an effort to try to heal myself, I started reading self-help books. That's when I first heard the term "life coach." It was life coaching that turned my life around. After reading what felt like hundreds of books on overcoming fear, finding your purpose, and healing your life. I read *The Mind, Body & Soul Diet* by Jennifer Nicole Lee. I was immediately inspired and moved by her story. She had overcome a lot and was now using her life to motivate and support others as a life coach and fitness instructor.

It showed me the power of courageously sharing your story. You never know who is listening or reading. It may be the one story that moves someone to change their life.

Reading Lee's story made me realize that what I had gone through in life could serve a purpose and inspire others. I knew right then that I too was going to become a life coach. I was going to make it my mission to help other women become more, get unstuck, and create a life by design.

THE COURAGE TO LIVE YOUR DREAM

To do this, I had to overcome my two biggest fears: what people would think of me and public speaking.

I learned through my coach training that my fear of public speaking stemmed from not wanting to be seen in the world, so it made sense that every time I was required to stand up to speak, I would go into fight-or-flight mode.

To overcome my fear, I invested in Toastmasters. I would volunteer for any duty that required me to stand up to speak. I'm still a member and continue to do all those things in order to improve my speaking skills. I also worked one-on-one with a speaking coach. Now, I'm excited for any opportunity to speak to groups of people.

I also realized that worrying about what people will think of me is a total waste of my valuable time. In fact, this fear crushes more dreams than anything else I see as a coach.

I knew it wasn't going to stop me anymore! I came to a point in life where that stuff didn't matter. It was no longer about me -- it became about the lives I could change or even save by sharing my story.

It was about being courageous and a little badass, all rolled into one. That's when my inner alter ego, Betty Badass, was born.

But if I was going to live life fearlessly, I knew had a choice to make. I could either continue to live in a ball of sadness based on my story or I could take responsibility for my happiness and be grateful for the things I did have.

I made the choice to be grateful for all the happy times my son, Chris, brought me, and for my beautiful grandchildren, Aedan and Halle, who I'm so lucky to have.

I made the choice to no longer let my story of abuse define me and keep me a victim. The minute I made those decisions, my life changed.

INVESTING IN YOUR GROWTH

As a result of my decisions, I began to value myself and see my worth, which led me to invest in my personal and professional growth. Committing to invest in yourself is the third key to living life fearlessly. We must place as much care into ourselves as we do for others.

I spend a lot of time and money investing in professional growth to be the best coach possible for my clients. I also invest in my personal growth and wellbeing by exercising regularly, reading inspiring books and spending time with Ron.

Today, my life looks very different than before. I'm different. It's now my mission to share these three keys to living fearlessly with the hopes of inspiring women to transform their lives and follow their passions.

Once you find the strength to let go of being a victim and move beyond your life circumstances, begin to courageously live your dreams and commit to investing in yourself, your life will begin to blossom.

Jason Russell

Jason is an I.C.A.N vitality specialist and author who empowers people to instill greater belief within themselves and take their self-confidence, health and vitality to the next level. He believes everyone has untapped potential waiting to be unleashed, such as losing 5-20 kg, improving energy for more important things like family, health or competing in fitness events.

Overcoming hormone difficulties, bullying, self-esteem issues amongst other things, Jason has come through a stronger person. He inspires people to break through their barriers and limitations to live a rich fulfilling and meaningful lifestyle.

www.icanvitality.com

✉ **icanvitality@gmail.com**

f **facebook.com/jason.russell.710**

f **facebook.com/pages/ICAN-with-Abundant-Vitality/268271839992267**

f **facebook.com/groups/1540033726233648/?ref=br_tf**

⊙ **#icanvitality**

CHAPTER 19

FROM BULLIED TO EMPOWERMENT

By Jason Russell

As we paddled our way in our canoes along the beautiful Bogong River in Victoria, stroke by stroke we got closer and closer to our destination. Our full class of students had canoed for hours on end, having fun exploring the amazing qualities Mother Nature had on offer. The wind gently blew through the trees and the sound of water splashing with every stroke. The adventure was made even more enjoyable as my canoe partner and I got along really well: between us we had packed an entire week's worth of food, which was in a bag with us. Craving a delicious sugar hit, we halted our progress, had some chocolate, and continued on our way.

When we got to our camping destination we set up our tents and had some food; among the healthy, delicious fruit and vegetables (which made up of about 10% of our meal), we hit up our supply of sweets! Oh the sugary goodness our brains told us we craved! Delta creams, multiple blocks of chocolate, Tim Tams – you name it, we ate it.

Wow! Things have changed since then and here is what happened since.

I always loved the great outdoors, as well as playing sports such as tennis and cricket, which helped me keep fit and active and fuelled the fire to exercise. I was always short growing up; people would look at me and underestimate my talent, so I would use that to my advantage during sports. It also gave me motivation to push harder and work harder than my teammates.

Whilst sport and recreational activities were highly influential, something that deeply affected me, especially during my teenage years, is a condition known as Kallmann Syndrome (KS). Even though it is defined as a physical condition, it is just as much of a psychological one as well. This condition causes several responses in the body, and I experienced an inability to create my own hormones, thus causing imbalances in hormone levels, delayed puberty and anosmia (lack of smell). I also experienced the feelings of being deaf in one ear, amongst many other symptoms. This is a rare condition with only 1 in 50,000 males experiencing it, and even fewer females.

During school I kept my condition to myself, building a wall so high and so thick that no one would be able to get in. I would not allow anyone to know. I didn't talk to doctors, family nor close friends, in fear of what people would say. Any negative comments, being bullied, being rejected – I didn't want it. I hated my condition, and I didn't understand it: I wanted to be someone else with a "normal body." I would ask myself night after night "why me?" and hoped that things would change in the morning.

The fear of people finding out gave me huge insecurities, which led to a lack of self-confidence, self-esteem, low self worth, and a fear rejection. The longer school went on, the thicker the shell and higher the wall I built. My goal was for no one to know about it, and I grew quieter not wanting to talk to anyone, which lead me to suffer from depression. I got bullied which lead me into the vicious cycle of hating myself even more. Bullied for being short, bullied for the way I spoke, bullied for just being me. I tried changing, thinking that other people would like me.

I went searching for acceptance, searching for something that others were not providing me with when they ignored me; until one day I realized that only one person could give me what I craved: myself. I realized that no one else would accept me if I did not accept myself first.

"Life is about 10% what happens to you and 90% how you react to it"

~ Charles R. Swindoll

Feeling isolated due to the condition, being constantly bullied day at high school, and also getting into fights during the last two years of high school created very low self-esteem, low self-confidence, low self-worth and self-hatred. I chose the best option that I saw at the time, which was to push people away and hide behind fears and disempowering beliefs. The final months of being bullied gave me fire to get into the gym and train to build up my size so that I could fight back and have a better chance of defending myself. I also did this because I believed that if I looked a certain way that I wouldn't get bullied anymore.

KS use to influence my life in a completely negative way: I had negative thoughts, which led to depression, and also used negative behaviors as coping mechanisms (such as isolating myself). I have learned now how KS has positively impacted my life, and I use this to my advantage now. It has given me so many opportunities that I most likely would not have been fortunate enough for, or realized their power, if I had not been through the trials and tribulations of KS.

"Nothing is neither good nor bad but thinking it makes it so"

~ Shakespeare

Having the condition is one of the best things that could ever happen to me. It has given me so many challenges and has helped me improve my mindset on a whole new level. I went from a shy, teen with low self-esteem, low confidence, & low self-worth, not wanting to talk to anyone, to now possessing the most self-confidence I have ever felt and can freely express myself with anyone, as well as discussing KS and its effects on my life. I am now inspired to help others reach the same level of self-worth that I have, whether their life has been touched by a medical condition or not.

"Self-worth comes from one thing, thinking that I am worthy"-

~ Wayne Dyer

I used to ask "why me?" Now I realize why I was meant to have this condition: to help inspire other people to push past their boundaries, push past their limitations and limiting beliefs. Your current situation doesn't determine where you go in life; it really is about what you do.

For me KS has been like a catapult, it has drawn me back as far as it can go, to the lowest of lows, for it to slingshot me to the highest of highs, at altitudes I never thought I would reach. If you don't like something, you have the power to change it, and if you can't, then you have the power to change how you think about it.

My motivation to train now has completely changed. I have greater self-esteem, greater self-confidence, self-worth, and I am passionate about helping other people with their goals. I don't train to defend myself in fights; I train because I want to be the best that I can be – training for fitness events, climbing the highest mountains, taking on any challenges and always improving my health and vitality.

> "Treat your mind, body and spirit like a temple.
> It's the only place that you must live in"
>
> ~ Jason Russell

Liana Bakker

An illness made Liana realize that she should live her life any way she wanted. Now Liana runs a blog that aims to connect people to each other through their stories of personal growth and triumph over adversity.

She also works with luxury vacation property developers where she helps them increase revenue by giving their clients access to antioxidant drinking water while helping the environment.

Want to be happier, healthier and more fulfilled? Check out her website to get some great tips, as well as read the stories of some amazing people.

www.lianabakker.com

f **facebook.com/liana.bakker**

🐦 **@itsallmolehills**

CHAPTER 20

YOU AREN'T YOUR JOB

By Liana Bakker

It was like a scene in a cheesy holiday comedy. Bad event, after bad event takes place right before Christmas pushing the lead character to near breaking point. Twitching with frustration she heads to the mall determined to finish up last minute shopping. She gets everything she needs and waits in the ridiculous line, pain from her recent car accident shooting down her leg. Limping through the doors with more than she can carry she realizes that she doesn't remember where she parked. There's a hole in her boot and her sock is wet. Trying to mentally retrace her steps she feels the rain soak into her thick sweater. The outdoor speakers are playing Christmas music as the icy rain pours down.

Mele Kalikimaka is the thing to say, On a bright Hawaiian Christmas Day.

The music blares; her body fills with rage.

Mele Kalikimaka is Hawaii's way, To say Merry Christmas, A very Merry Christmas to you!

"Does this look like f***ing Hawaii to you?!"

She didn't shout, but definitely said it a lot louder than intended. People walking by looked at her like she was crazy, except the guy jingling those annoying little bells for the Salvation Army who stopped mid "Merry Christmas" to stare. He started with a small chuckle that eventually turned into full-blown hysterics. She stared at him angrily for a moment and then burst out laughing herself.

This is where the cheesy holiday movie ends.

If it had continued she would have started cackling like a character played by Jim Carrey and then tackled him to the ground. Maybe she would use the pennies he collected as projectiles to stop the good Samaritans that were holding her back.

Luckily, I just stood there laughing. I saw the humor in it.

"Bad day?"

"More like bad week…" I found a dollar in my pocket and put it in the bowl.

"Thanks. Merry Christmas."

"Merry Christmas"

I took a good deep breath to clear my head and the location of my parking spot came back to me. I hobbled my sopping wet self back to my banged up car. It felt like my life was falling apart and the things that I was once proud of accomplishing seemed meaningless.

In just one week I had been given a cease and desist letter over my business name, my office building became uninhabitable due to a fire and I was in a head-on car accident. It felt like the universe was screaming, "STOP! Stop and look at what you're doing. Re-evaluate and change." Although I did believe that I needed to make changes, I didn't have time for that nonsense. I needed to write next term's lessons for my students, find time to see all of the patients that I had cancelled, find somewhere permanent to set up my business, get my car fixed, go to physiotherapy, make money to pay my bills.

I didn't have time to slow down, let alone stop. So, the universe decided to send something else my way. A bone infection in my mouth and face. After the ordeal of dealing with the acute infection, I still found my energy to be quite poor. I worked very few hours and spent the rest of my time sleeping or lying on the couch watching TV.

Bone infections don't exactly feel amazing, and one night in particular was really bad. I was exhausted, but in too much pain to sleep. I got up out of bed in the middle of the night, sat on a pillow on the floor and began to meditate. I sat there trying to calm my mind and body. I began repeating positive things about myself: things that I didn't

125

even really believe but wanted to be true, things about my health, about who I was, about my life and my finances. I sat in the dark for 3 hours talking to myself in a calm zoned out state.

By the time I was done I felt like a whole new person. Something inside me had changed. I suddenly believed all the things I had been saying. I also had this overwhelming sense of knowing. I knew the only thing that would ever really make me better would be to start living the way I imagined I could. Or at the very least, I had to try.

It was hard at first to shed my baggage of how I thought things were supposed to go, and look at what I wanted if those things didn't matter. So I created a vision of how I wanted my life to be. Not just goals, but a way I wanted my life to feel. I decided that I would start making efforts that moved me closer to that vision.

Although I loved my job as a Registered Massage Therapist, I knew that I wasn't living with the freedom that I had always wanted. I also knew I wasn't helping people in the best way I that I could, so I set out to start a new business that would give me the freedom I craved, as well as a blog aimed at helping people through tough times.

In the beginning I was too tired to really do anything. I spent my time listening and learning. I watched videos, read books and took online courses that would teach me some of what I needed to know. Even as I became healthier, progress was slow. I started to wonder if the vision I had created for my life would ever come true, and I doubted my ability to make it happen. I started to think that the epiphany I had was false. I saw people around me moving at speeds much faster than I was, and they were doing things I didn't feel ready to do.

But I realized that I had this idea that success is only measured by the numbers in the bank account. Most people do. When we introduce ourselves to new people, the first thing we tell them is what we do – the thing we do that makes money. Although this is an easy way to start a conversation with someone, it doesn't really tell what kind of person you are.

You are more than just your job. You are more than just the dollars in your bank account. The amount of Twitter followers, email subscribers or contacts you have isn't the only interesting thing about you. Your promotion, your corner office, your new car, your all-inclusive two weeks in Fiji aren't who you are. Yes, these are all successes, but they are not the only things that make you successful.

Small victories and wins in your daily life that move you toward the vision you created are successes as well. The small steps you take that move you towards the way you want your life to be are worth celebrating.

"I will be a success only when I have completed everything that I have ever dreamed of accomplishing!"

What about everything before then?

When I was really sick, eating healthy all day was what I considered success. As my health improved, I added layers to my small achievements creating a new meaning for success.

Most people set large meaningless goals and think that when the big things are complete they will feel successful. Instead, create a vision for your life and then set small efforts that lead you to that vision. Each time you complete one of those small goals you are a success.

It's not about having everything figured out; it's being dedicated to the time and effort it takes to get to that point. Many people give up. If you stick with it, then you already have a success story.

Now, whenever I feel doubt in myself, I remember the vision I created for my life and think of the things that I am grateful for that fit my life's vision.

I have healthy relationships. I took the time and effort to heal my body. I realized that I could do anything I want with my life and am taking small steps to make that happen. I run a successful massage therapy practice, and I am trying to help people connect with the world around them. I am willing to face adversity in an effort to build a life filled with freedom and travel.

These are successes.

I am a success.

Jessica Ledet-Bellard

Jessica Ledet-Bellard is a certified life coach, motivational speaker and entrepreneur. She has written many articles and manuals on how to balance life and work, platform building and living on purpose. Jessica has been honored with many awards including Humanitarian of the Year, Inspirational Entrepreneur of the Year and more. She has traveled the U.S. sharing her message of living life on purpose and not allowing anything to dim your light. Jessica is an advocate, inspirer and educator who enjoys sharing her life experiences in hopes to help someone realize that being in the wilderness is not the end.

CHAPTER 21

TRIALED AND TESTED, BUT NOT DEFEATED

By Jessica Ledet-Bellard

An energetic and intelligent schoolgirl, filled with hopes and dreams of being a well renowned physician, she was blessed in so many ways: a supportive family, scholarships, colleges calling and more. What else could she ask for?

That girl was me, but little did I know what was about to transpire. My life was about to change drastically before my eyes, in ways that I never imagined. At the young tender age of 18, I was a freshman in college enjoying this newfound life of being an adult, and I was finally figuring out how to activate my faith on my own.

It was until that one rainy, stormy morning that I awoke and for the first time could not even stand. I lay knowing class was starting in the next hour, wondering what was wrong and how I was going to make the mile walk to campus. As I prayed for the pain to subside and for strength to get up and get moving, I couldn't help but wonder what had gone wrong.

The day before I was full of energy, happy and full of life... now what? I finally decided to push past the pain and take a slow stroll to campus. As I sat in class I wondered what could be the problem; I never experienced this type of pain before. The professor finally closed her folder and ended class, and I slowly got up from my seat and made my way to the hall, immediately calling the doctor. I had never been so happy in my life to hear a doctor say, "Yes, you can come in today."

As I sat on the exam table I couldn't help but think, "I am only 18, just beginning this life with my heart set on being a doctor, what am I up against?" I remember reminding myself of my faith and knowing that God could heal me of whatever it was.

After my exam the doctor turned and looked at me and said I would need to have a laparoscopy to explore the problem further. He assured me I would be okay, but there was something in me that needed more info, so I researched when I got home. My research wasn't going so well because the Internet can be helpful, but also scary.

I had the procedure and one week later I went in for my follow-up. I was told that I would most likely never have children and that endometriosis was covering most of my female organs. The surgeon assured me I could live life just like any other female, and he had done as much as he could to help. All I could do was take pain medication as needed.

I remember leaving and wondering what was next for me, I felt as if I was alone and my life had ended. I was no longer happy, vibrant and full of energy I was depressed and filled with anger. I could not understand what was going on and how it happened. I always loved and cared for children all my life and the thought of never having my own was devastating. I sat in my apartment crying and praying to God for answers.

Needless to say this was only the beginning. A first semester college freshman, with an illness with no cure, living in pain with no hope of ever being a mother. Devastated with no definite answers, I want back to school in pain each day wondering when it would end. As time progressed the pain returned and intensified, grades begin to fall and I began receiving notice from my scholarships that if my grades didn't come up, they would take my scholarships away.

I sat in my apartment and cried every day, not knowing what my future held, sinking deep into depression. I felt as though my dreams of being a mother and a prominent physician were so far out of reach. I began to immerse myself in the word of God, and it was at that point I found strength, strength that I never knew existed. I finally began to realize that God was a healer, and he could truly turn my situation around.

Two years later, as a junior barely hanging on, I was faced with my second surgery to remove cysts and more endometriosis, causing me to set two semesters out. Although, my faith had been strengthened over the years, I couldn't help but wonder, why again? I felt as if nothing was going right. My scholarship was taken and my only hope of finishing college was to find another means to pay.

Bruised and battered but not defeated, I picked myself up and continued to fight. Then on my birthday that same very year I received the most spectacular news: I was expecting! Excited and nervous, I left the doctor's office. As I sat in my apartment I remember thinking, can this illness affect my unborn? Is there anything special I need to be doing? Will I be okay?

Nine months later I welcomed my firstborn into the world. Proud would be an understatement if I had to explain the feeling. I knew God had an awesome plan for me. For the next 6 years I cared for and nurtured that baby to best of my ability and continued to go in for my yearly appointments. Six years later God blessed my husband and I with yet another baby. I remembering screaming out, "Look at you, God!"

The second miracle was just as wonderful as the first. As we sat in awe of our two beautiful blessings that God had given us, we couldn't help but rejoice. Little did we know just a few months later we would receive a call from the doctor saying we needed to come in. Hesitantly, I drove over to the office and the doctor began to explain that my results from my annual were not favorable, my heart fell.

She told me that cancerous cells were showing. My eyes immediately began to fill up, and I couldn't help but wonder what this meant for my young family. It was at that point she said I would need another surgery to try and remove the cells. As I explained the situation to my husband, he immediately began to cry. I remember encouraging him to pray that everything could and would be removed in surgery. The surgery was a success, but I would have to be examined every 6 months now to make sure the cancerous cells didn't return.

Little did I know a third miracle was under way. Mackenzie, our third child, was welcomed into the world one year later. The house was really coming to life! I was graduating college and everything seemed to be turning around for us. Then BAM! The pain was back and in full force.

I drove myself to the doctor's office demanding that something be done. My doctor referred me to a specialist who knew exactly what was going on and took me to surgery within a week. He did extensive work inside removing my ovary and tube, repairing adhesions and cleaning everything out that needed to be out. Relief was finally in place, relief that I had never known – a new me. I could now be the wife, the mom, the student, the friend that I always wanted to be.

Through my continual research of the Bible, I began to study the story of the woman who suffered for 12 years with a blood issue; she reminded me of myself. After 12 years of not really knowing much, I began to research ways to help myself and others deal with this condition that was barely spoken about. I began to examine natural remedies and looking for other women who suffered from this ugly and tormenting disease.

It was at this point that I decided to take my 12 years of torture, depression and agony into my testimony. Women S.P.E.A.K, an organization that advocates, educates and empowers women all across to globe to learn more and be tested was birthed. I have chosen to be the voice of the unheard millions who can't or are afraid to speak. I have chosen to turn a life filled with pain and hopelessness into triumph.

Reyna Joe

Reyna Joe is from Curaçao. She is a journalist, communication services consultant, writer, radio and TV personality.

Class and professionalism is her long-term project that started in 2009 with her writing and speaking for different young professional organizations and using the information acquired during 25 years of running her own company.

She uses her writing in a continuous effort to create awareness about certain professional topics and pushes for the class and professionalism concept to become a tool next to all diplomas, perfect grades and what one already knows, in order to survive careers.

CHAPTER 22

WHAT THE DIPLOMA DOES NOT ASSUME

By Reyna Joe

I have been blessed, as I was raised in a time and country where girls were expected to go to school, to get a diploma, and to work to take care of themselves. Any girl. No restrictions.

I am even more blessed for having lived up to these expectations, raised in a supporting family where I was made aware of the role I had to play as a professional. Yet, around me, I see that many, who also had the opportunity to study, have lacked additional information and guidance in their development.

Having a diploma does not mean that you are done, sufficiently prepared or professional. It simply means that you are equipped with the minimum ability and brains to learn, understand, and apply a skill based on some standard of measurable performance.

ABOUT CLASS AND PROFESSIONALISM

After 25 years running my own business and handling my own HR, I tried desperately to motivate young professionals to give it their best. It did take some time for me to understand and accept that it is where you come from that determines if you will be a professional, regardless of your diplomas, and the lack of the basic social tools to survive in the working environment might be the single biggest culprit of underachievement in the workplace.

In my business I had too many young "professionals" squander opportunities and jeopardize their professional life due to lack of manners and other basic social skills.

In short, too many "intellectuals" do not know how to behave. It made me understand why so many "professionals" are only qualified to be back-office workers, unfit to be taken out in public professional settings. They do not even understand why their career is not progressing, why they are only invited to an event once, why attainable career opportunities seem to melt away and why their contract is not prolonged.

I have had many conversations with young professionals on this topic. The impression I always get is that there is a lack of understanding on how to behave professionally, which means people lose opportunities to move forward because they fail to realize that proper manners will open doors.

And there's more: being professional shows in the quality of the work you deliver, the effort you exert beyond the strict requirements of your contract, the attitude you have, and your general manners.

A lack of the right manners and not being conscious with your work becomes a professional and social trap. Caught in it, you either are removed or shoveled away with the rest of the deadwood. Gone is the power of your good grades if you do not have proper professional manners. I am not talking about brown nosing. Keep in mind that you can be extremely critical, even rebellious, whilst being well mannered.

The biggest challenges to otherwise capable young professionals are:

- Coming from a home where he or she is the only child who got the chance to finish college/ higher education
- Coming from a home where none of your parents had a higher education
- Coming come from a home with one or both parents working for foreigners and they affirm that those are the real authorities to be respected and to work for
- Coming from a home where the main income source was social welfare
- Coming from a home with a working mother who is not around

- Coming from a home where the word "protocol" was never used
- Coming from a home where you were motivated to study and where there was no way of knowing how to guide you later in the professional workforce

In addition to knowing the rules of behavior at work, you must accept that your backpack with social information has to be emptied and refilled.

- No, your mother cannot visit you at work.
- No, your father cannot call to ask you to go run an errand.
- No, your lover cannot come and sit and watch you work.
- No, you cannot dress the way you want.
- No, you cannot add your CEO on Facebook. Seriously.
- No, you cannot change the rules at work to make them fit you.
- No, your boyfriend cannot call your boss to explain why you should not do specific tasks.
- No, you are not going to ask your boss to dance with you at the company's reception.
- Yes, you must know what they hired you to do.
- Yes, you have to earn the right to be listened to.
- Yes, you must follow the work rules.
- Yes, the office hours as indicated are the *minimum* amount of work you have to do.
- Yes, you are a representative of the company even outside of working hours.
- Yes, there is a difference between you and the hierarchy at work.
- Yes, you must leave the company behind better than how you found it.
- Yes, you love your family, but no one else is related to them.

Empower yourself, your career and your future with the right protocol tools, which are listed below.

- Learn the rules of professional protocol
- Learn how to be in the organization that hired you
- Join people who are willing to support you in your career
- Find a mentor
- Work on how you speak the languages you know and work on how you talk
- Do not let others introduce you in official situations. Do it yourself on the first day you start working or when you arrive for a business event
- Work on your self-esteem
- Know your place. When to talk. When to shut up
- Be discrete or just quiet if you do not know the difference
- Inform yourself on the dress code and develop your own professional style. Err on the conservative side
- Participate in company events, professional events and work on your contacts. Those business cards you got at work are to be used and shared
- Realize that a company/organization is a micro community in your community. That means that you meet all kinds of people
- Keep telling yourself that you are a professional and play the role according to your specialization. Your workplace is your stage
- Keep educating yourself in the highly competitive world where everyone with a diploma wants to move upwards. Everyone looks great on paper
- Educating yourself today does not mean that you have to leave your place or space to know more; the Internet is the fastest, safest, surest learning place
- Keep reminding yourself that the right professional attitude determines if you succeed at staying or not
- Be a team player and learn from your teammates/colleagues. Teach them as well.

- Keep the environment where you work pleasant
- Say thank you. Mean it.
- Keep your workspace clean and neat, do not bother colleagues with the multilevel network business you just joined, maintain good personal hygiene, do not gossip, respect everyone, and treat everyone respectfully, especially if you do not like them.

So to get the best out of you, for you, after your diploma: accept that you don't 'recover' from your class because of your diploma.

And you have the choice to reinvent yourself and get maximum benefit from the investment made in you.

REFERENCES

Author's 25 years observations of professionals in work situations

Dr. Mariano Heyden II Lecturer in Strategy & Business Policy, Newcastle Business School, Australia

http://makebalance.com/not-fitting-in-with-the-corporate-climbers/

http://www.parenting-healthy-children.com/whyiseducationimportant.html

http://voices.yahoo.com/breastfeeding-helps-children-social-ladder-208344.html?cat=25

http://voices.yahoo.com/the-influence-social-class-education-90543.html

Kuumba Nia

Kuumba Nia works with heart-centered business owners to create and grow successful businesses from a place of self-knowledge and self-mastery. Known for blending the principles of authentic leadership, universal law and energy alignment tools, Kuumba delivers simple ways for entrepreneurs to reignite the passion for their business, so they can step up to the challenges they face or step out into something new.

Kuumba is the author of *The Circle of One: How to Heal Your Relationships and Live Your Truth;* co-author of *Success in High Heels: 30 Day Feast to Success;* a Reiki Master Teacher and qualified Executive and Leadership Coach.

www.kuumbania.com

 facebook.com/kuumba.nia

 twitter.com/kuumbania10

 linkedin.com/in/kuumbania

CHAPTER 23

IT TAKES PRACTICE TO REMEMBER WHO YOU REALLY ARE

By Kuumba Nia

It was my pride and joy.

Founded on a desire to provide the space and guidance for people to grow emotionally and energetically, the Centre for Holistic Personal Development was my creation, the next step in my evolution, and a source of real pride and comfort to me.

Aesthetically, it was pleasing to the eye. Energetically, it was an oasis of calm and tranquility – a place to reconnect to self and Source – and I loved it. More importantly, I loved who I had become in order to create it.

I was clear, confident and sure of my direction. I honored the space I occupied; I cleared the energy regularly, and valued the contribution I made to others above all else. Faith and spiritual focus were my guides, and for me, it was all good.

Then something changed.

After years of steady growth, and the growing belief that anything was possible, the economy suddenly came crashing down around us. Costs rose, client numbers fell and endless fears and insecurities about the future started to creep in. Or so it seemed.

The truth was that, in my case, it was the doubt that first appeared and then the flow stopped. Creating the dream of the Centre was one thing, but, as the reality of running a brick and mortar business hit me, I could feel the anxiety rising. Working with clients was one thing, but this business of business seemed to call for something more than

I had. Unsurprisingly, it wasn't long before my ill-judged decisions, mocking doubts and misplaced trust, all served to undermine my confidence. Before I knew it, I was in a downward spiral and the closure of my beloved Centre was imminent.

When the time came, it was incredibly painful. The sense of grief and loss was huge. Not only had I lost my business and my spiritual base, but I felt as if I'd lost my identity too. I had no one to blame but myself.

How had I let it happen? Was I really cut out for this or had I just been fooling myself? Maybe I didn't have what it took to run a business. Maybe I just wasn't good enough.

And although I never really allowed myself to dwell too deeply on those questions, in the back of my mind, I had already come up with the answer. It was simple. I just didn't have it. Sadly, even though I had arrived at this conclusion, I never articulated it. Consequently, the thought, the belief just sat there, constantly present in the background, consuming me like a cancer, feeding on my doubts and eating away at my core.

So what happened next was hardly a surprise. Careful to avoid my earlier mistakes and caught up in the belief that it was my lack of business acumen that was responsible for the closure of the Centre, I went from one extreme to the other. I decided that my approach needed to be more 'earthy' and less 'energy'. I clung to the belief that all I needed to do was to learn this stuff. I clung to it for two years, certain that if I had the marketing skills, the business know-how, the mastery of numbers, it would all be fine.

It wasn't.

I had missed out one crucial factor: My business was people. My business was energy, and anything that didn't take that into account was doomed to failure.

I was and still am, one of life's energetically sensitive people, and any way of being in the world that doesn't allow for the expression and expansion of this side of me, just doesn't work. Any path that departed from my soul purpose of remembering the beautiful, joyful, carefree spirit that I truly am was not going to work.

Somewhere in the fight with myself to prove that I wasn't some kind of 'business retard', I had forgotten that. I had forgotten who I truly am; why I was here, the difference I was here to make and the lives I was meant to touch.

My spirit however, had not, and the misalignment between how I was being and how I needed to be, left me feeling miserable, exhausted, and at times, practically unable to function.

There were days when the pain of disconnection from myself and the separation from Source reduced me to a sobbing heap. My spirit knew, even if I didn't.

And yet I still carried on. Not sure why, or even how, I just did.

But I needed more than tenacity. Perseverance alone wasn't enough. I knew I needed much more. And that's when it dawned on me. One morning as I walked around my favorite park, I looked up and noticed my surroundings. I mean, really noticed.

I noticed the myriad of shades of green; the birds singing, the squirrels jumping and the astoundingly beautiful, rich shade of azure blue that hung reassuringly above me. That was when I knew what was missing. I needed to renew my connection with Source. I needed to make energy and spiritual practice central to my life and my business, just as it had been when I started the Centre; when forgetting was never an option.

If I was ever going to recover from this, I had to go back to what I knew, what had prepared me for this journey and what would carry me through if I let it.

So that's what I did.

I made a decision. I was going to choose deliberately, every day, to feel good. What that meant in practice was that I had to change the way I felt. I had to feel good about myself and my business before there were obvious things to feel good about, which meant I needed to feel good most, if not all of the time.

Slowly at first, with fits and starts, stumbles and falls, I began a daily practice. It was nothing too onerous or impractical, just a daily ritual of writing things down.

There were 3 very simple things that seemed to have the most impact on the way I began to feel.

The first was to reconnect with my joy, to remember the things that made me smile. Things I'd heard or seen, someone I'd met or even the memory of my children as babies. I looked for the evidence that there were good and positive things in my life and I listed them. Everything I could think of, from the smallest to the greatest, I wrote them down. That was when I started to notice just how abundant my life was already.

The second was to really experience gratitude. To appreciate the little things that showed up: a rainbow, a compliment, children's laughter, or just that I woke up that morning and the sun was shining. Soon it was a new client, a contract, a refund.

The third thing was to deliberately choose what or how I wanted to feel that day. The list could be as long or as short as I wanted, as long as it was made up of strong positive emotions.

As the days, weeks and months passed by, I took every opportunity to listen to audio, watch videos and read books that raised my spirits. I went to workshops and invested in courses and programs that challenged me to be more – anything that would help me to see the joy and the abundance that I already had around me. I walked in the park, I sang out loud; I smiled at the beauty and innocence of babies, and I felt appreciation for every wonderful moment. It didn't all come at once. But every day, I could feel the momentum gathering as I felt better and better.

My daily practice has grown since then, and first thing in the morning, I do any number of things that make me feel good, before anyone can steal my joy.

145

I've come a long way since the close of the Centre and I know I'll go a lot further. Life is good, and as you'd expect, I judge my successes and failures in a very different way nowadays.

For a long time I pursued success on other people's terms, believing that if I didn't do it that way, or get those results, then I had failed. What I know now is that the real failure is in not trusting my own knowing and allowing myself to forget.

For me, real success is about being aware, authentic and true to yourself; it's about deliberately choosing to create a life filled with ease, joy and appreciation and helping others do the same.

Ultimately, I see success in its purest form: as the reconnection to self, to the joy of remembering who I really am and living that, as far as I can, in every moment.

I guess by that measure, I truly was born for this.

Anne-Marie Brungard Knight, MBA

Anne-Marie, the Passion Project Strategist, has truly found and stepped into her unique sweet spot in the world. Unleashing all of her gifts (from engineering and business education to social service management experience) she has created a proprietary system - The Passion Project Blueprint - to support visionary business owners and social change agents design and build their Passion Projects on time, on budget and on mission, so they can embrace their heart's mission and make an impact in the world. Anne-Marie is a fourth-generation entrepreneur, wife, mother, grandmother, avid camper, trainer, speaker, coach, real estate investor and glamorous cupcake baker.

www.PassionProjectStrategist.wordpress.com

- Anne-MariePP07
- 1-203-503-8994
- PassionProject07@gmail.com
- facebook.com/AnneMarieBrungardKnight
- facebook.com/brungardknight
- facebook.com/Transform.KingdomBusiness
- @PassionProject7

CHAPTER 24

FROM SECRETS AND SHADOWS TO SANCTUARY AND SHINING

By Anne-Marie Brungard Knight, MBA

"This little light of mine, I'm gonna let it shine. Let it shine, let it shine, let it shine."

The first time I heard this song, I was seven years old and riding my brand new bike down the street. Although I just wanted to ride and ride, the singing stopped me in my tracks. But where was it coming from? "This little light of mine..." the singing got louder and louder as we approached. They sounded like angels. And there it was, the one room Sunday School with 60 children crammed onto 30 chairs. Their faces shining, smiling and that sweet singing, "Let it shine, let it shine, let it shine!"

My sister and I were invited in by the man in the blue uniform with a squeeze box in his hands – the sole accompaniment to the singing. We were hesitant. There was no way we were leaving our bikes outside. A missing or stolen bike was definitely not something we were willing to explain to our parents. "Don't worry," Brigadier Drake said, "we can pull them in here." Trust me when I tell you there was no room for the two of us, let alone our bikes, but they made it work. Before we knew it we were squeezing ourselves onto crammed seats and took our places in that glorious choir. I'd found my place, my sanctuary.

The Salvation Army gave me a place to be and a place to grow. It was a safe place. That kind Brigadier and his wife made weekly visits to our home for tea with my mum. He always had a magazine for the adults and a pocket full of candy for the neighborhood children. Our Salvation Army Pied Piper did not know, he could not know, and could not have imagined the secrets behind our closed doors.

I remember one evening as I put my head around the corner of the kitchen, a cold feeling settled into my stomach and my heart started racing. I knew something was wrong. I could hear banging and bumping sounds. I peeked gingerly around the corner, my heart stopped. My mother was on the floor, her eyes full of fear. I could see one hand holding her down and the other gripping the knife at her throat. I could hear my own heartbeat, ba bump ba bump. I stretched my neck just a little further only to gaze directly into the eyes of my father, the man with the knife.

Frozen in place, my eyes widened and my heart stopped. He spoke words I will never forget: "Annie, I'm not hurting your mummy. I love your mummy." With the same smooth Queen's-English-Jamaican-British accent that I knew. No change in tempo or tonality. "I love your mummy." Even at three years old, I knew that didn't make sense. That somehow the words did not match up to the picture burned into my memory. Somehow, I think the fear in my mother's eyes cancelled out the "love" part.

I lived at the crossroads of Secrets Boulevard and Shadows Avenue for most of my life. We never spoke about what happened at home. I would go to school every day – singing, skipping and smiling with the other children – and no one knew. The oldest child in a home riddled with domestic violence. Always on guard, watching and waiting for the next event. Maybe dinner wasn't served on time or the carrot juice wasn't just right.

There was always some "good" reason for my father's actions. My mum dealt with the physical and emotional scars, although I too have carried emotional scars. We ran away once and ended up in a shelter. Four of us squeezed onto one set of bunk beds. Mum disguised in a wig and different clothing to be able to leave the shelter in safety. She cried every night. We had never been exposed to anything like the shelter before. This wasn't what she wanted for us. We went back home. Even though I pleaded for her not to.

When I was eighteen, we packed up and ran away for good. The undercover operation required precision planning and timing. Passports. Check. Money. Check. Transportation. Check. Airport security. Check. At 7 am my brother and sisters were being given the news that we were leaving. We could each bring one suitcase. I left my job, my friends, my neighborhood without so much as a backward glance. One day I was working as a draftsman at a fabulous job on Euston Road in London and attending college full-time; the very next day I was in a new country, around new relatives, looking for a new job and starting a new life.

My mother always taught me that I was stronger than I thought I was. In school I learned that I was smarter than anyone ever gave me credit for, and, life taught me that that the safety and sanctuary I longed for was already inside me.

Fast forward through a career in engineering, ministry and non-profit management, and through one marriage, two beautiful children, one divorce, grandchildren and foster parenting. I could also slow down and linger for a while about my breast cancer diagnosis, treatment and now 23 years cancer free. We could have tea and chat about the impact of addictions and finding new love. But what I really have to say is this: I am finally living free. I am no longer hiding. You will not find me peeking out of the shadows. I am no longer afraid to be who I was born to be, who God made me to be!

How did I get here? Great question.

All my life I never quite fit in. I just discovered – down deep inside of me – that I was never meant to fit in. I would try and bring homeless people home for dinner as a child. I took the technical drawing classes at school, as the only girl in a room full of boys. I was the one black kid in the group of white kids. When other kids were playing dress up, I was hammering and building with bits of wood on the construction site with my father. I was always different. This realization alone changed me completely. I don't think like everyone else. I dream big dreams. I don't do small...never have. My dreams were what kept me sane when I was surrounded by madness. My dreams gave me life and hope. Where I was stuck was in my thinking. I believe it is the most widely read book in the world that says, "As a man thinks in his heart, so is he."

When I finally hit that point when I was really sick and tired of being sick and tired; you know, that place where you are tired of struggling, that place where you feel empty but full of promise, that frustrating place where you can still see your dream and you are clawing your way uphill to reach it. Yes, that place. That place where secrets and shadows no longer serve you. That place where you must step out into the light to feel the warm sunlight on your face to breathe! Yes, that place. When I got to that place - I got up and got help. I hired a coach to help me grow my business. What I didn't expect was how that relationship would help me grow me!

I am a fourth generation entrepreneur and I have always known that some day I would have my own business. This is my family legacy. I consider myself a serial entrepreneur. From a gift basket company, to a gift retail store, and from a training professional to a business consultant, I have tried, tested and fallen flat on my face at times with several businesses. Each trip and fall made me more determined to get it right, to work it out. The thing is, each time I did get back up!

Although I was re-positioning my business, I had to take a look at ME! Any stumbling block could usually be traced back to my negative money mindset – the fear of not having enough; or my fear of stepping out from the shadows; or my lack of trust in people's words and actions. Do you hear that word FEAR, FEAR, FEAR? Fear kept me bound up and locked down, fear kept me ducking, bobbing and weaving away from the next metaphorical hit. Fear kept me hiding in the shadows.

In order to achieve success, which for me looks like a life of Shalom (peace - nothing missing and nothing broken) from relationships to finances, I had to change my mind. Replace old thinking with new paradigms, new ways of thinking. I had to see who God saw when He looked at me. I had to decide to consciously live my life in the light, unafraid to share my gifts with the world.

Changing my mind changed my heart. This is work, let me tell you. But for all we have been through, this is a gift we can give ourselves. When the little voices in the back of my head start talking back to me, "you can't do it," or "you won't make it." I shout back: "I am worthy. I give myself permission to have all that God has planned for me. I give myself permission to accumulate wealth, as it supports my purpose in life. I give myself permission to be safe. I am safe."

This is not an easy journey, but it is worth it. I am worth it! YOU are worth it. My life's experiences and gifts are now aligned to serve others in my own unique way, which is who I have always been. And now I can truly let my light shine!

Julian Bongo

Julian Bongo is an experienced global financial markets professional, entrepreneur, inspirational speaker and African diaspora activist originally from DR Congo but raised in London. Julian is a keen practitioner of investments in the emerging markets of Africa, having previously held a variety of senior positions on development projects.

In addition, Julian holds a Master's in Finance and investment management diploma from the London Business School. He is currently a risk manager in the banking industry and a keen motivational speaker, inspiring audiences to get out of their comfort zone and turn failures into success.

f **facebook.com/Mrjulianbongo**

🐦 **@julianbongo**

CHAPTER 25

THE PRICE OF SUCCESS

By Julian Bongo

In 2008, post the Lehman collapse and as a result a global financial meltdown, like many people I found myself jobless, losing my apartment and returning home to my parents. Although largely caused by the global financial crisis, my personal crises were as a result of bad management and fast life style. This phase can be explained in many different forms, although my failures started way before 2008, in fact, ten years prior.

I came home from work to find the love of my life had packed up and left me, leaving a Dear John letter on our dining table. The dining table where we once shared meals, planned a future and had our collective friends over. The letter did not clarify the why; all it said is that we were through. It felt like I had been shot in the head. As I sat on the couch I tried to justify to myself what went wrong. Just like the crash of 2008 it did not happen overnight.

I would like to draw from my experience on how personal relationships' success or failure has a direct link to how we perceive our overall success or failures in life. Everyone can be successful, but in order to value your success, one has to know what the failure trigger was. In my case the real trigger was the impact of the breakdown of my long-term relationship. Now did I stop to deal with this? Oh no, I decided to throw myself into my career and business.

During this time, I was at the top of my chosen career in investment banking and started to invest into various business ventures. These became my tools of choice for distraction from the crash that was my personal life. I had managed to attain relative success in the form of a small global property portfolio, coupled with a jetsetter lifestyle. I became known as Mr. Playboy and was very popular in my social scene of high flyers. I had resigned from my role to begin an MBA program, but failed to adjust my life to reflect the changes I was going through. This is where the fuse was lit.

Ever since the breakdown of that relationship, I had found myself in doing mode, not stopping to fully assess or reflect on the situations that I was facing. Instead of accepting that something had to change, I kept on going till I hit a brick wall. I found myself jobless, losing my apartment and returning home to my parents. My personal crash had blinded me to facing the reality as I was working and operating with my head in the sand. How did I get here?

My journey to this point was all my own doing. I was a man using my career as a crutch until I found another crutch. My lifestyle became my biggest distraction, and trying to live up to my playboy persona, I started to neglect my businesses and myself. The dedication and drive that got me that success had fizzled up and died away. My graduation from business school in 2008 coincided with the collapse of Lehman Brothers, and I had a great job offer withdrawn from my previous employer. The entire job market was in meltdown causing a global recruitment freeze. For the first time I found myself unemployed and broke.

The situation didn't get any better for months, resulting in property repossessions and defaulting on various commitments. Failure was finally steering me right in the face; in fact, it was the face I saw when I looked in the mirror, this wasn't the life I was accustomed to and it drove me to a mild depression.

I finally realized that the success I had experienced was built on weak foundations. Not dealing with my internal concerns had clouded my mind and lead to a series of poor decisions, which landed me in this place I called "failure."

If nothing else will push you to change life, pain will. I knew something had to give.

Pain drove me to soul searching, tapping back into my spiritual side and staying still for a while. During this phase, I identified that for things to change; I needed to change how I viewed myself and the world around me. I had to get honest with myself and stop feeling like a victim. My failure was largely due to poor planning and lack of flexibility at point of changes in circumstances. Most importantly, I had failed to respect who I was and what I stood for.

I reminded myself of a quote I came across years ago: "If you stand for nothing, you will fall for everything." So I started asking myself some key basic questions. I knew I had to change.

First the mind. I started to appreciate the people around me. The support of your inner circle is key when going through major life changes. Most of my failures were as a result of not considering the advice of people who have my best interest at heart. I embarked on a quest to rebuild relationships with those I valued in my life.

I also reconnected with my spiritual side to further enhance this new experience, and I committed to being more involved in my loved ones' lives. I decided to start a physical training regime to strengthen my body and physiology.

Secondly, I decided to take basic steps to address my finances to better manage old debt, as well as current commitments. I created a strict financial management plan. This was not easy, as in the process you can feel exposed and judged by your peers and associates. This is when I had to return to place of humility and be humble about everything I was going through.

Thirdly and most importantly, I decided to open up and deal with my emotions, which I had allowed to change me and my behavior towards women. I didn't want to love anyone, but welcomed casual relationships. But this was not me. I shed tears looking at myself in the mirror one morning, as I felt empty, despite having a long list of digits to call if I wanted company.

This was the straw that broke the camel's back for me. I spent time speaking to those whose opinion I value about my feelings and state of play. This helped me a great deal, as I began to realize that I wasn't alone and I was a victim of my own imaginary reality. I made my issues much bigger than they were, and therefore sunk in the darkness for years by holding these feeling inside in the hope that they would sort themselves out.

Each one of us has experienced failure at some point in life and will in the future – that's for sure. The great news is, failure is the best tool at your disposal to become successful in everything you do. Although subjective, it serves as a reference point or springboard to project you to success. Use it wisely.

Success can be quantified by material and personal achievements, to the extent that the emotional and personal costs are often ignored. Years prior, a combination of personal relationship dissatisfactions and my inability to address fundamental attitude flaws had pushed me to put all my energy and passion into working as hard as I could. During that time I was able to build a comfortable living standard and gained access to a great global network of associates.

Behind every success story is an embarrassing first effort, a stumble, a setback or a radical change of direction. It's these first clumsy steps on the road to success that fascinated me.

Sara Donovan

Sara is a management consultant who is passionate about helping her clients integrate their heads with their hearts. After fifteen years designing and facilitating workshops on neuroscience, influence and innovation, Sara utilized these skills to pursue a long ignored personal calling – creative writing. In 2014, her romantic comedy novel, *Love By Numbers*, was published by HarperCollins Australia and debuted as an iBooks bestseller, and Kobo's Best Reads, before being selected by Amazon US for their "Unforgettable Fiction" list later that year. Sara is currently writing her second romcom, while teaching creative processes that help people unlock an understanding of and commitment to their personal callings.

www.saradonovan.com

www.saradonovan.com

iBook – bit.ly/1kBd8rL

Amazon – bit.ly/1kBdoqU

Kobo – bit.ly/1rZF0pS

facebook.com/saradonovanbooks

twitter.com/sarasbooks

CHAPTER 26

THE CREATIVE UNIVERSE PLAYBOOK

By Sara Donovan

I am a wife, mother, performance consultant and author.

My debut novel is enjoying its second consecutive week as a bestseller on iBooks Australia, which is kind of fulfilling and also hilarious, because of course that only happened when I stopped caring whether it did or not.

There are so many contradictions when playing the Creating Game, the 'Don't be attached to What You Want Even Though It's Super Important to You' principle being one of the most perplexing.

Add to that the 'Law of Reverse Action' (the harder you try the less progress you make), and the Outcomes Paradox (to get outcomes you need to forget about outcomes), not to mention the feelings of utter disillusionment you usually have to face when creating something you really want, and it's not surprising that people get stuck somewhere on the road to creating and let their dreams fade.

Or at least, that's what happened to me. It took me 40 years to begin my passion project because I didn't understand the paradoxical nature of creating.

My dream job when I was a teenager was scriptwriting for TV or film. The thought totally floated my boat. I couldn't think of anything more fun. Or scary. Whenever I got bad marks for essays or stories I thought were great, my enthusiasm would deflate like a popped balloon, and I'd be left with a deep sense of shame about not being good enough, which was disproportionate to reality.

By the time I left school, my lack of emotional resilience and my oversensitivity about being evaluated led me to decide to have a career in science instead of writing. While I found my career in science very stimulating, I regularly confessed to anyone who would listen that I had a fiction book in me. The conviction and hopelessness in my voice when I said that was always confronting.

Ten years into my science career, my children were born and I started a business writing and delivering corporate training programs using science, specifically neuroscience, to help people understand their behavior. It was a big step towards creating something important, but I still felt pregnant with a fiction book that I really wanted to write but couldn't start.

It took another ten years before I found my way to a fiction writing course and immediately hit obstacles – my first drafts were awful, my ideas weren't original, I wasn't funny like the other students and the shame I felt about not being good enough, was as real as ever.

I interpreted my returning negative emotions as evidence I had no talent and that my writing dream was just a childhood fantasy I needed to forget.

Which I would have done, except for one thing.

Envy.

My author envy became so severe that I couldn't pick up a fiction book and read the back cover (let alone a chapter), without feeling a mountain of angst and confusion as to why I would be so attracted to something I believed I couldn't do.

Fortunately at the age of fifty, after not reading a fiction book for years, my angst became so heavy, I realized it would be less painful to push through my debilitating fear of not being good enough and just write a book anyway.

I did, and had the most exhilarating and enlightening ride of my life. There really is nothing as freeing as finally accepting your calling with no regard to the outcome.

But it needn't have taken me so long. I could have learned earlier how to handle the paradoxes of creating, which is why I've written the Creative Universe Playbook – a list of paradoxes and strategies that can help navigate the counter-intuitive nature of creating your deepest intent.

The list isn't complete, but my Creative Universe Playbook helps me understand the rules of the Creating Game and reap the greatest outcome – a recreated, more compassionate and free me.

1. THE 'WANTING' PARADOX

Secrets

Not all wants are equal. Some wants are a desire to correct a symptom rather than a desire to solve a problem. These are Reactive wants (e.g. if only I had... then I'd be worthy). They are an avoidant want, don't satisfy and lead to more Reactive wants. Creative wants are a desire to express the self (e.g. I want to... because it floats my boat). Problems are overcome on the way to creating the vision.

You can tell the difference between Reactive and Creative wants by how they feel.

Reactive wants feel like longing, frustration and impatience. Creative wants feel tranquil, satisfying and patient.

What you think you want often isn't what you *really* want. The creative game isn't ultimately about fulfilling your dreams. It's about who you become as you fulfill your dreams. This is how you change the world. By changing you.

Strategies for Managing the Wanting Paradox

1. Notice the amount of longing or angst your Reactive want creates.

2. Meet the want like you're meeting an equal. Don't be intimidated or ashamed or annoyed by the want. It's just programming in your mind.

3. Write, write, write your uncensored Reactive wants. Be welcoming and gentle of them even though they cause you angst.

4. When the Reactive wanting eventually tires of its own story, invite your deepest intent to speak to you.

5. The voice of your deepest intent is more subtle than your Reactive want and will feel tranquil, compassionate and wise. Write, write, write your deepest intent. Notice the effect it has on your body – hang out with it. This subtle part of you knows how to hold a want lightly and trust the creative process.

2. THE 'DOING' PARADOX

Secrets

There are two types of doing: obsessive doing and harmonious doing.

Obsessive doing is when you struggle to walk away from a task because your need is compulsive. You can still create an outcome in the short term, but the 'Law of Reverse Effect' means the more you try the less progress you make. The destructive cycle of effort, burnout and effort freezes the creative flow, leading to inconsistent results and suffering.

In contrast, harmonious doing is when your actions flow from your body's knowing, which, in turn, flows uninhibited from your unconscious mind. When creating from this place, reality with all its challenges is not resisted or judged. This allows for even more freedom, creativity and of course, better results. Your action has a spontaneous flowing, and in that sense is effortless.

Strategy

1. Become a spectator of compulsive thought, striving and struggle.

2. Set the intention for the mind to let go of itself, then go and do something fun.

3. Notice when you get ideas out of the blue that make sense, are compassionate and energizing. Follow them.

3. THE 'RESULTS' PARADOX

Secrets

The most effective way to bring about results is to *love the process* and not care about results.

This can seem like the biggest paradox of all – investing your time and energy in pursuing something and not caring whether you get results or not. Yet for an outcome that is out of your control, like getting a job you love, finding a partner or coming up with a new business idea, this paradox is critical.

Strategy

1. Identify and appreciate the deepest intent your desired outcomes represent.
2. Identify and appreciate the process you are going through as you express that deepest intent. Notice how this helps you relax about outcomes.
3. Observe the outcomes you want with curiosity. Notice you are holding them loosely, neither choking them nor giving up.
4. Hold outcomes lightly and with curiosity until they are either fulfilled or replaced.
5. Appreciate every result that shows up.

4. THE 'DISILLUSIONMENT' PARADOX

Secrets

Being disillusioned occurs when the problem you are trying to solve is too complex for the current version of operating system your mind is running.

The strategy

Get in control of your self-talk. If you tell yourself that being disillusioned is a sign that the Creative Universe isn't supporting you, then you will churn frustration and move into more reactive states. Your energy will be spent coping with the frustration of not getting what you want, instead of being used to overcome obstacles and moving towards your deepest intent.

Prime your mind for an operating system upgrade by sitting with the uncertainty of not knowing and seek resources to support you until you understand the answer.

Finally

Paradoxes and wisdom date back to the ancient Greeks. But it isn't just philosophy that lays claim to contradictions. They are well documented in physics, logic, math, economics and the cognitive sciences to name a few.

Paradoxes are perplexing and at first appear to be mistakes. But even as the mind wrestles with them, paradoxes feel right, open our mind, relax our body and are beacons lighting our deeper knowledge of ourselves and the benevolent Creative Universe.

Kojo Bonti-Amoako

Kojo Bonti-Amoako is a speaker who specializes in helping people find lasting fulfillment from within in all areas of their lives, careers and relationships.

His career spans over 15 years in coaching, training, media performance. Kojo Bonti-Amoako has advised several brands, been a voice over artist and public speaker, worked as media planning director and as on air broadcast presenter, and in 2007 co-founded Sunlight Radio in the United Kingdom, which was sold to the Infinity Broadcasting. He currently serves as the Chief Executive Officer of soon to be launched Fantastic Radio in London.

CHAPTER 27

CHALLENGING YOUR CHALLENGES
By Kojo Bonti-Amoako

Life has an interesting way of re-introducing us to ourselves daily. What I mean is that we discover ourselves every day; that is, if give ourselves the opportunity to make that happen. As we travel through life, we are bound to encounter challenges that have the potential to sway us off course in our lives – things that I choose to call challenges!

I first of call them challenges because the labels we use really determine how we respond to situations. The word "challenge" has several definitions, and the description that resonates with me is "to engage in a contest." I see life as a contest with ourselves and I constantly look at ways I can engage with the universe to maximize my potential. Instead of retreating and throwing the towel in, I looked to see what was in the box of life.

It was a fine Saturday afternoon with my wife and my 8-month old boy a few years ago. My wife asked me to feed my son, so I took him downstairs for lunch. We were downstairs when I heard my wife coughing, and I felt something must be wrong, so rushed upstairs to check on her. Something wasn't right, and I quickly called the ambulance.

We spent some time with her before she asked us to leave, as she felt our son was tired. The plan was to go in the following day to see her because the doctors were running tests and getting her settled. We got home on that evening around, and as I was settling our son I got an urgent call from the hospital asking me to come back in, as my wife had been rushed into intensive care.

It was a harrowing sight to see her placed on life support. The doctors mentioned that they are doing everything possible to save her life.

But after what seemed like an eternity, the doctor and two nurses told me, "We are sorry Mr. Bonti. We are so sorry. We could not save your wife!"

I had become a widower and a single parent in one cruel sweep. I was so devastated and heartbroken thinking, "How am I going to raise an 8 month old boy without his mother? What about the business we started?" I was grief stricken and fearful, constantly looking for answers.

I had a choice to cave in and start blaming the world or I could accept that my wife had passed and pick up the pieces and make the best out of what I had been presented. I chose the latter option, as I had a son to raise and a life to continue living.

How do you start picking up the pieces when your life falls apart? Friends. Dionne Warwick was right when she sang, what's friends are for? Good friends are just priceless! My good friends became my rock; they supported my son and me when we needed it the most. I had incredible people step up to help me with an 8-month-old baby while I struggled to grasp the intricacies of single parenthood.

Friendships should never be taken for granted. It's vital to develop relationships with good people and invest time to grow these relationships. Having good friends allows you to be yourself and not be afraid of being judged.

YOUR LIFE NEST

On a wet winter's morning I was pushing my son in the pram on our daily walks in the woods, and we stumbled onto a bird's nest on the ground with a bird in it. I wondered where its parents were, particularly its mum. How could they have left it to defend itself? After a long walk we came back down the same path and something fascinating happened. As we approached the nested the bird hopped to edge of the next and took to the skies.

It quickly struck me; the bird in the nest at the time we were passing was facing a challenge of its own: take to the skies or be eaten. It chose to soar. It's interesting how we can sometimes find ourselves in situations where we keep going round and round and think we are not making progress, just as the baby bird I saw. I believed whilst it was going round and round in the nest it was plotting and planning, setting its eyes on where to go when it left the nest.

I went through a similar situation after my wife passed away, where I woke up, fed my son, took him for walk – the normal routine parents do. But one day I thought to myself: what would I do when my son turned five and started school? I decided to invest my time wisely so that as soon as he was old enough to go to school, I would have choices and opportunities. I did a whole lot, and today I am reaping the benefit of it.

What are you doing with the time you have? That time that seems nothing is happening? Do you want to try a new course, a hobby or planning for your own business? You would be very surprised what you can achieve when it seems like you're just in a nest going round and round.

YOUR LANDMARKS

When I was fourteen years old, my late grandfather said to me, "life is not against you and everything that happens to you, I believe it is not to destroy you, it is there to make you a better person not a bitter person." This has become my mantra. There will always be situations in which you find yourself, making you feel trapped with no way out. These challenges that come your way to help you grow, not to destroy you.

If you take a closer look at your life, you will notice landmarks events and periods that have challenged you. How you deal with these challenges will help you on your road to success. These experiences are stepping stones that you can use in challenging your challenges; it does not have to be huge. Out of the challenges you can find the strength to make yourself a better person and grow even if you have to fail forward!

The past few years have been very tough, and I have learned so much about myself, how my mind works, who I am as a person, a parent and, most importantly, how to appreciate life and the good people around me.

My son is now 6 years old and is a well-adjusted young child; something I am very proud of. I wish you all the best and success in your endeavors and may spot your landmarks to draw strength from when you come across challenges in life.

Conclusion

Everyone falls down and you are not alone. Everyone experiences failure. What we don't see in that moment is that we are failing forward. This simply means that even though we have crashed and burned, we have also moved from where we started.

It is possible to recover to start again, just like a phoenix that rises from its ashes transformed and brand new. You can do the same and transform your journey. My deepest desire is that this book acts like a catalyst to transform your journey to success.

I can honestly say that going through the process of creating the book has changed how I view myself and what is possible for me and each of the co-authors who stepped up to the plate to share their story and pour a part of their souls into their chapters.

We are not alone in walking this path, and we are more than we know. With that said, success is not a singular destination, rather more of an evolving state of being that changes over time, and one that keeps changing and growing. Be gentle with yourself knowing that though you may fall off the path, you can always stop and take a moment before getting back in the saddle on your journey to success.

Call to Action

Are you ready to elevate your journey to success? Is now the time to step out and take center stage in your own life?

I would love to help you on your journey to success in your life, love and business! If you would like to learn more about coaching, speaking and services provided by Lillian Ogbogoh, do visit www.lillianogbogoh.com

The End

CPSIA information can be obtained at www.ICGtesting.com
Printed in the USA
BVOW01s2136090315

390922BV00019B/359/P